SOON
I'LL BE FROM
THE SOIL
SOMEDAY ESSAYS
ON PLANTS
AND LOSS

ELEANOR AMICUCCI

ISBN: 978-0-578-39080-2

Typeset in P22 Stickley Pro.
Design and typesetting by waynekehoe.com

Contents

Pressings..6

Lavender...12

Aloe Vera..34

Pruning..44

Trees...55

Sunflowers..79

Perennials...85

Propagation...96

Cut Flowers..110

Evergreens..114

Jade..122

Compost..135

Buddleja..144

Reminders..159

Acknowledgments..161

About the Author...165

For my sister, Carrie.
You are a bright light, you are beauty, you are a creative wonder.
You are your grandmother's granddaughter.

Pressings

CLEANING OUT Dede's home more than a year after she has died should feel more morbid than it does. I expected that going through someone's belongings, especially the belongings of someone I love and miss, would feel eerie and uncomfortable, but it does not. It feels warm, cozy. It feels like Dede.

Dede was my grandmother, my mother's mother, and she died last summer after years of illness. She passed away peacefully just shy of eighty years old, after a full and gorgeous life. A life that mattered, a life that touched others in profound ways, a life that changed her pocket of the world. A life like every other life before it—an irreplaceable and necessary part of this Earth, ever impactful, forever a piece of the puzzle that is this strange and stunning planet. Gone in one form, yet still here in others. Always guiding, always present, even if only through the mesmerizing glow of silence.

Her death was one of the most beautiful things I have ever been a part of. She knew before she died that her time was near. I did not ask her how she knew, though I can ascertain. Dede was, like me, a trained ballet dancer, and we shared a similar fascination with the human form, its complexity. Even as her body weakened in her later years, she still wanted to learn about and practice stretches, movements, anything to feel whole and balanced in her bones. She understood the beauty of the human body, and was deeply in tune with her own.

So while I did not ask her how she knew with such assuredness that she was going to die (*I have a few days left*, she said, and she was right), I am certain it is because even in her demise, she had a keen awareness and love of her own body, and it told her when it was ready to finally rest. Our bodies are always speaking, if only we choose to listen.

When I was younger, I would do anything not to feel what was happening in my body, in my mind. Life didn't make sense to me, and I wanted nothing to do with it. If I had to be a part of it, I wanted control. I did not want to ride the incessant wave of emotions that coursed through me—I wanted to direct that wave. If my mind was an ocean, I wanted my body to be the moon—pulling, shifting, eternally guiding. But it is impossible to control the ephemeral, impossible to harness feeling into something lasting.

Over the years, I have learned that the only real control comes from letting go, from relaxing the grip on my own life and understanding that I am not the moon, nor am I even a boat in the ocean of my mind. I am more like a buoy. Bouncing, bobbing, submerging, momentarily sinking, but ultimately always floating onward.

I become like the buoy by being like Dede, by learning to embrace my body. For so much of my life, I lived exclusively in my own head. Though I studied ballet daily and practiced other physical activities, I was never present in my own skin. I never wanted to be. To be wholly alive is to experience pain, and I did not want that—so I hid. What I did not realize during the hiding process was that to be alive is to also experience pleasure, joy, love—and to hide from the pain meant hiding from the beauty too.

You can't be selectively present, a healer would tell me later in life. I know this in my bones, and yet sometimes I try to hide, just from the moments I fear. Presence is a practice, and the only way to be truly human, truly alive. Presence is always, happening, now. I am still learning this.

When we go to clean out Dede's house, it does not feel the same as it did when she was there, though the smell remains. I bury my face in her clothes and inhale her. I start to cry. I cry in this moment not because the smell reminds me of her, though it does, but because I had been so afraid that after all this time the smell would be lost. That distinct Dede scent, musky and warm, forever evaporated into the ether. But no, here it is, waiting for me. So I cry, joyful tears, full tears, tears that remind me I am alive and present and whole. I continue.

In the upstairs of Dede's house is a vast collection of books. I find a few to take home with me. A copy of *Nureyev*, gifted to her by me many years ago. A Russian language book for beginners. I find a copy of *Women Who Run with the Wolves*, a favorite of hers and mine, and put it in a box. I find three hand sculptures made of metal, two a faded white and one a rich brown, each gestured in a slightly different position, and I snag these too. Tucked in a corner of the room I spy a green velour mannequin head, eyes shut and head tilted. I think of Dede, how we all lovingly mocked her because in every photo she's ever been in her head is tilted, leaning toward the person next to her. Always yearning for a captured closeness. I take the mannequin head too.

After perusing the rest of the upstairs, I think I have gone through it all, or as much as I can muster on this trip, until I come across an object that calls out to me. Two rectangles of wood, secured together with four long screws, full of sheets of cardboard and paper towels. The whole thing is light, cannot weigh more than a pound. On the cover, in green capital letters: FLOWER PRESS. I begin frantically unscrewing the contraption, desperate for a glimpse at whatever might lay inside.

I am flooded with memory. Bright petals between small fingers, smushing plant bits onto pages and screwing, twisting, securing the top on until it is firmly shut. Never to be seen again, until now. Here, this twenty-five-year-old me holds the fruits of the labor of my much younger self, a child who worked in tandem with her now-dead grandmother to preserve something beautiful, something lasting.

Inside I find several flowers, each one more translucent and fragile than the last. When I take them home, I attempt to find some way to display them. Each is sectioned between two sheets of paper towels, and removing them from the paper proves impossible. I think about simply gluing the towels down to larger sheets of paper and framing them like so. I think about laminating it all into one piece, protected in a sheath of plastic, immortalized. I think about commissioning someone to create something marvelous, to take that which is long dead and revive it, to make art from these phantom flowers.

In the end, I do none of these things. I gingerly compile the sheets of paper towel, place them between the two wood slats, and screw the whole thing tightly back together. It sits next to me on my bed now, memories awaiting my retrieval, ready at my leisure.

In pressing flowers, we cannot save anything. We cannot prolong a life. By the time the flower has been situated between the pages of a press, its life cycle has already been completed. It is dead. And yet.

There is beauty in the translucent and decades-old flowers, a little gift from the past to the present. There is beauty in the uncertainty of not knowing where to place these works of art. There is beauty in the death that I hold between my fingers, and there is beauty in letting go of that, of not trying to make it into anything more. There is beauty in saying: everything I love must die, and everything dead has its place.

I thought visiting Dede's home and collecting her belongings would be morbid, but it is not, because I am already steeped in morbidity. I am thinking about, constantly pondering, death and dying. I am trying to find the good in it. I am trying to be like leaves in the fall and let go with ease and forgiveness. I want to remember who I was before loss, and I am trying to see if it's possible to reach back that far, before remembrance.

In pressing flowers we cannot save anything but ourselves. Though the flowers die between the pages of the press, little pieces of oneself are kept alive. The memory of a smaller me, a more tender version of myself, holding onto flowers with wonder—she gets to live on because of the sacrifices of leaves and petals. My grandma, a woman who sought beauty everywhere and brought it with her wherever she went, can live on through the press, through what she and it taught me. How to honor life, how to cherish it in all its forms. In pressing flowers we cannot save anything but ourselves. If saving does not mean living, if even in death there is salvation, then in pressing flowers I am whole.

This is what I am attempting to do here, on these pages. I know that in writing I cannot save Dede—I can never bring her back to life. I also know that in writing I cannot save myself. That even if my words are immortalized on paper, I am still very much human, animal, mortal, dying, soon to be dead in the grand scheme of things. I am decaying. I will be gone. There is no saving me, in the literal sense. And yet.

There is still value in compiling thoughts, in noting lessons. This year has been so strange, full of loss and full of love and especially full of plants. The quietest living things. The plants have shared with me this year, opened my eyes to a different way of being. I want to press those lessons onto these pages in the hopes that one day I can open up this book and find a gift from my past self. My present self. From me. And maybe that will be enough.

There is no saving me, not in the literal sense. One day I will be reading these words and I will know, just as Dede knew, that my time is near. I will read these memories, these lessons, these pressings, and know that I have lived a full life. I will tell my children and my grandchildren *I have a few days left*, and I will know it with certainty. Because I will no longer fear my body, because I will understand it. Because I'm listening.

For now, I sit here, still young and uncertain and learning. I am writing and I am pressing everything I know so far—everything the plants have taught me, everything loss has given me—into paper. I am not trying to hold on. I am not trying to change anything. I am simply here, witnessing, giving to an idea of beauty I have yet to meet. In saving these thoughts for later, in recording these words for whoever may find them, I attempt to honor the natural world that I am a part of, to witness it and to love it, exactly as it is. There is no slowing down the wheel of life, but we can clasp it in our hand and examine it, like grains of sand or a fallen leaf, and know that when we are ready, it will be okay to let go.

Lavender

To be a lover of peace is to be a lover of lavender. There is not a scent in the world more calming, more grounding, than that of heady lavandula. Long sprigs dried and crushed between fingers, a sachet tucked between folded clothes, fresh flowers plucked from a shrub, oils distilled for rubbing on wrists or spritzing onto pillows, soy candles lit in moments of stress or before sleep. I love her, desire her, in every form.

In Italian, lavender is *la lavanda*. It grows better there—in Italy—than at home. Native to the Mediterranean, it thrives in dry sandy soil with maximum sunshine. Despite its origins, lavender has traveled the world, and has been cultivated into varieties that can withstand a wider range of climates. It adapts to survive—it is wanted everywhere, and so it must morph or perish. Still, even the most diverse lavender varieties have the same basic needs, and the plant will not perform if those needs are not met. I have been trying not to resent lavender for existing exactly as it does. I am trying not to resent myself for doing the same.

I move to Italy soon after Dede dies. The plans had already been in the works for months, and though I toyed with the idea of staying home after she passed, I ultimately decided to go. It felt silly to stay—she was already gone, and not going to Italy would not bring her back. In her final week alive I told her about my trip to Florence, how I wanted to go there to look at art and eat pasta. I showed her pictures of the apartment I found, one in the heart of the city with a patio full of plants. I was drawn to the quiet alive things long before I understood why.

Dede asked me what I wanted to do for a job once I got to Italy. A career counselor and headhunter by trade, a business founder and owner from a time when only men held such titles, I knew these things held great value to her. I didn't know how to explain that while I'm grateful for the progress she has made for womankind, career has never held much appeal to me. It's a means to an end. So, I told her—honestly—that I had no idea, that I didn't care. I wanted to live, wanted to spend time in my favorite country, the country of my people, and more concrete plans about money and the future would only stand to get in the way.

I spend a month in Florence, looking at art and eating pasta and mourning. I cry more than I think possible. I flail. I am terrified. I am in one of the most beautiful cities on Earth and yet it feels pointless, feels like a lonely and pitiful waste. I do not tell anyone this. I tell people I am happy. I tell people I am eating lots of gelato and practicing my Italian (true). I tell people I am grateful I am here (untrue). I feel cranky and miserable and spoiled and alone. I miss Dede. I want to hold her hand one more time. I want to tell her I think I made a mistake in coming here. I want to call her from my apartment, sitting outside amongst the flowers, crying, and confess I'm having a hard time. Everything is perfect and yet my heart aches so deeply, and I don't know what that means. Is there something wrong with me? Will I ever be happy? Will I ever just be okay?

I want her to comfort me, I want her to center me, but she is gone. I am alone in a foreign country, a country I possess citizenship to and yet I know is not truly my own. I know I do not belong.

Dede was not Italian. She was Russian, and deeply proud of her country and culture. Though she did not live there, Dede kept Russia in her heart all her life—chairing balls in Manhattan for the Russian Children's Welfare Society, attending and getting married in a Russian Orthodox church, and sharing countless stories of her family and history with those she loved. It is a punch to the gut to realize, remember, I will never again hear a story from her lips.

When I was young, I would silently will her to invite me to one of the balls. I was desperate to be a part of one of the magical nights I had heard so much about. I have been regaled with endless tales of my grandmother renting a suite at the Waldorf Astoria for her and her friends and making a whole evening of getting ready there before heading off to the event. I wanted to see it all, participate in what seemed like the pinnacle of fantasy, the height of glamorous living. *Bring me to the ball*, I would think, staring at her with sharp and pleading eyes from across a kitchen counter. In my mind, Dede was like God—capable of hearing my deepest desires without words.

When she died, the Russian Children's Welfare Society posted pictures of her on their social media pages to honor her. They quoted the obituary that my mother wrote, one that makes me cry to this day if I read it in full (my ability to write comes from my mother, and hers from Dede). Part of me, the little girl who never got to go to the ball, is mesmerized, so floored by the utter specialness of this woman who helped raise me. She is so important that this organization honors her in her death. That's my grandma, I want to point and say, to everyone, to you, to her. Her blood runs through me (this is reason enough to love myself).

Dede's love of Russia, of its people, was a central tenet of her being. I always admired this, the way she held her country in her chest everywhere she went, breathed it out with each exhale until the warmth and breadth of her love filled the room. I was not able to relate to this love of place until my first trip to Italy, when I lived in Verona for one summer while in college.

I visited Verona for a month, studying Shakespeare and Italian and falling in love for the first time with the Earth underneath my feet. I did not know it, that that was what was happening, this love affair with dirt. But I felt it there, in sweet Verona, for the first time: grounded. I felt my feet on the Earth and I knew:

this is right. I am right here, and this is where I am supposed to be. When I left Verona, I cried for a day.

I feel trite mentioning my tears so much, so often, peppered everywhere, but it's the truth of the situation. I cry. I cry right now, as my fingers touch the keyboard. I am always crying. Not always, not really. But enough. I think it's important to note this thing that our bodies do for release. I used to be afraid of crying, afraid I was falling in or out of control, afraid I would be devoured by the saltwater, wholly consumed by the liquid pouring from my eyes. Over time though, I have learned that my tears are here to hold me. That if I let myself feel my sadness, really feel it and process it in my body and let the tears flow, then it can pass through me. I need only be afraid of my tears if I fight them. I am fighting my feelings no more.

I cried when I left Verona because I had finally found a place that felt like home, and it felt like the cruelest, most unjust thing in the world that I should have to leave that. I returned from this trip and went to Dede's house for a visit. I told her I finally understood—I had found my place. I told her this excitedly, that I could see what Russia was to her, what it felt like to be proud of where your family is from.

Dede was not Italian, but my grandfather is. My grandfather, my father's father, was never someone I was close with when I was young. Grandpa Amicucci. Dispatched to Florida—a wise man, avoiding the blustery cold of the Northeast in his retirement—we never saw him much in childhood. However, after my trip to Verona, our relationship has flourished. We have found literal common ground, a deep and mutual love of the same patch of Earth: our sweet *Italia*, a country we are both now citizens of.

Where in the United States citizenship is doled out on the basis of *jus soli*, or by right of the land, in Italy citizenship is awarded based on the principle of *jus sanguinis*, or right of the blood. *Jus soli* means that anyone born here on American soil is automatically made a United States citizen, regardless of their parents' country of origin. *Jus sanguinis*, however, means that where you are born does not matter. So long as your blood is Italian, you are given access to citizenship.

The application process for those with Italian blood is mainly a formality, but a lengthy one, and from the start of the process to when we are finally granted citizenship takes several years. Grandpa Amicucci, *mio nonno*, pays for the attorney and the process. He gifts the whole family citizenship, birth certificates from Rocca Pia—the small village in the hills of Abruzzo where my family comes from—and passports in the rich red of *Unione Europea*. It is the greatest gift he will ever give me, the opportunity to return home, to finally feel my feet planted in the ground and to know that I can call such a place my own.

When I return from Verona I know I cannot ignore this, this feeling in my chest. The Dede-Russia feeling. The understanding of: Oh, this is where I come from, this is the place that has shaped me, created my family, crafted my bones and breath. I breathe in, I breathe out. I see. I understand. And so, I know I have to go back, I plan to go back. I plan and I work and I save money and I plan and I am ready to go.

And Dede dies. And Dede dies, and it shatters everything, more than I thought it could. I knew for years that she would die, knew for months that it was imminent, and yet it still catches me by surprise, still shakes me. I do not want to face it, the reality of it. The humanness of it. The death of it all. I wish then that I could have left sooner—that I would have already been gone before she was. Life has other plans, and Dede dies two weeks before my scheduled flight. No haze, no avoidance.

Lavender came into my life several years prior to Dede's death. It did not appear before me as a flower, nor as anything recognizably alive. It came to me in its distilled form, its essence. Oil condensed into an amber bottle. I discovered this plant in essence form at trauma camp.

"Trauma camp" is not the real name of a place I go to. It's the nickname my fellow patients and I lovingly gave to an inpatient trauma program in the middle of the Arizona desert. I ended up there just after I turned twenty-three, and several months after an incident that left me agoraphobic and PTSD-riddled. A stranger harmed me, profoundly, and I became a shell of a person. I gradually stopped going to school, stopped socializing. I could barely leave my apartment, and every sound, every movement, had me on edge. I decided it was better if I died.

Before I did, I gave myself one last chance, one opportunity to heal. Trauma camp. I went. I attended therapy all day every day, and gradually came back to myself. Found myself anew. But it was not simple to get there, and I wanted to give up many times over. One of the therapists told me while I was in a particular funk: *There is no silver bullet for this. There is no one person who is going to heal you and make this all feel better. Only you can do that.*

I wanted to punch him in the face when he said this, this cowboy-hat-wearing loud-talking pseudo-spiritual-seeming man telling me I wasn't trying hard enough, I was waiting around for someone else to fix me. I wanted to punch him in the face because he was right, and it was true, and I knew it in my core. I knew that, despite all my greatest wishes, no one else was going to heal me. For so much of my life I wanted that—wanted someone to swoop in and make everything all better. As a child, I never felt protected and never developed any sense of security, in myself or in the world. And here was this man telling me that no one was ever going to give that to me. That protection, that sense of safety. No one but myself.

I did not stay angry long. Some part of me—the part that knew there was nowhere to go but up and that I would be the only person to carry me there—tried. I tried with everything I had, gave healing my all. I became closer with the women I was living with, realized we were all suffering, and all had the potential to heal.

I had panic attacks almost daily at trauma camp, though they subsided over time. It was funny, in a way, to go from having panic attacks in my apartment in New York City to having panic attacks in the middle of the desert in Arizona. They became much more expansive in the wilderness. There was a freedom found in screaming toward the open air, and even in what felt like the death throes of a truly horrible panic attack, there was something healing about experiencing it with my feet firmly planted in the sand. During one of those panic attacks, I fell to the ground, cowering from an imagined predator. I tumbled into a bush of cacti and watched the look of pity on a nearby friend's face. I have never been one for pity, and even well-intentioned sympathy makes me uncomfortable. I have always struggled in accepting a helping hand.

After this particularly bad panic attack I was approached by a woman who lived in the same building as me. She'd heard about what happened, and she wanted to help. I was learning to accept the assistance of others, learning to admit the limits of my own knowledge, my own capacity, and so I accepted. She pulled out a small bag, offered it up to me. I do not remember what she said, what words were exchanged between us. All I remember is holding out my wrists, her rubbing a rolling ball dispenser in circular motions against my skin, and breathing in.

I am certain that I had smelled lavender before that moment, and yet it was never the same before, nor after. Never before did I understand the true power of the plant, its full capacity to heal. It is because never before this moment had I needed it so much. Plants always show me: when I need them, there they are.

That beautiful breath in of lavandula feels too good to be true, except it isn't, and it never is again. It is always true, it is always exactly as I think. I am smelling lavender as I write this, and I am trying to find the words to explain its scent. How does one describe the scent of a flower when flowers are so often the reference point for everything else? "This lavender has hints of lavender" does little to paint an image in one's mind's eye (mind's nose? Does such a thing exist? Can we smell with only our minds the way we can create images in our head? I need answers).

The woman from trauma camp told me I could use her oils

whenever I needed, and suddenly she had inserted hope into my life. This angel sought me out of her own volition. She gifted me the ability to calm, to finally mellow the storm that was my mind and my body with only the power of a plant in my palms. In this moment I was shown: the universe is alive.

Falling in love with lavender was helped by the fact that it is already my favorite color: purple. Some will argue that certain, or even all, varieties of lavender are a shade of blue, but I refuse to believe it. Lavender is purple. Anything else is a travesty.

I think of the other purple plants I know and love, wispy angelonias and frustrating but gorgeous petunias, scaevolas and sweet Russian sages and alliums and hyacinths and orchids and salvias and lobularias and ornamental cabbages. There is certainly a plethora of purple available in the garden, and yet none move me quite like lavender.

I get greedy with lavender. It feels luxurious to me, and I want to hoard it. I become a collector, wanting to hold it and devour it. I buy candles, my own roller balls full of the stuff, and a perfume featuring it. I purchase lavender body scrubs and a lavender pillow spray, and a pretty purple sleep mask stuffed full of dried lavender that I never wear to bed, but instead lay with propped on my chest as I write and read before sleep. It is too heavy, too impractical to actually wear to bed. Defeating the purpose of oneself—halting and causing insomnia at the same time— is a special feat.

While for years I utilized lavender in its various forms, I never actually attempted to grow—or even learn about—the plant itself. I never even thought about it as a plant, as something that does grow, that has roots. In my mind, lavender is always detached from the Earth. I see the flower, I see the stem, but beyond that I am not interested. The foliage, the root system, what do these things matter if I cannot get that sweet whiff of those fragrant flowers, if I cannot transport my body into a field in Provence with a single inhale?

It is not until I move back to Italy, until after Dede's death, that I am finally confronted with the plant itself, face to face. After spending a month in Florence, I move to Venice. I find a family to live with and work for as a nanny. I had been to Venice once prior, on a day trip during my summer in Verona, but I had never spent any extended period of time there, had not seen the city outside the usual tourist traps. I head to *Venezia* by train in early October, coasting through Northern Italy until we arrive at the lagoon, where the train pulls us over the water and into the station.

There is no way to explain Venice until you have been there, no way to capture what it really means to live in such a fairytale-esque setting. My first trip there was overwhelming. I remember most of all being hot, regretting wearing pants, feeling generally sticky and crowded and unpleasant. This time is different. The family picks me up at the train station in their boat—the most efficient way to get around—and takes me to the island of Giudecca. If the main island of Venice is hectic and crowded Manhattan—with *Piazza San Marco* as the obvious Times Square equivalent—then Giudecca is Brooklyn: a calmer, more residential, less chaotic island.

I fall in love with the island, and the home. A red house, with a big yard and garden space that is unheard of in Venice—a city of apartments, not homes. I live in a small house on the property, *una casetta*, and my windows look out directly onto the canal. I imagine opening the front door and diving into the water, though I never do.

I learn to match my sleep to the water sounds. In New York, I became accustomed to city sounds—blaring sirens and honking horns, screams and daily protests coming from Union Square. A perpetual insomniac, this became my nighttime rhythm. In Connecticut, the unbearable quiet of suburbia was too much for my loud bedtime mind, and so I turned to the comforting drone of the television to keep myself aurally settled.

In Venice there is no honking—no cars!—and no protests, and there is certainly no silence. There is water, and there are boats on the water, and there are all the sounds that accompany this. Water is life, water is the womb, water is the great bathtub that is our planet that we're all floating and chilling and living and dying in. Water is, in a word, everything. But I never knew water to be particularly noisy, never understood just how alive the water itself is. Living here changes this. I learn every curve of the water, come to understand the sounds different boats make as they pass through it, the way voices bounce off the surface and birds come to linger and chirp near the canal's edge. Water becomes my companion, my only friend. I am utterly alone in Venice.

I know why I am here. I have returned to Italy because it feels like home. Home in the United States, home in Connecticut, there is too much baggage there, too many years of pain and miscommunication. It feels messy. I am desperately seeking family, seeking a place where I belong, and I move continents to find these things. Having arrived here, I can feel something gnawing in my stomach, pulling me home. Real home. The home where I grew up, the home where my parents live. The home I have always rejected.

At the Venice *casa* there is a large garden, one that only the grandfather of the little girl I care for tends to when he comes to visit. The greatest feature in the garden: a large lavender bush, maybe three feet tall and wide. At the time, before I know enough to think of it, I do not ask which variety of lavender it is, how old it is, if it blooms well. Now I wonder.

While I'm there in the fall and winter, little is in bloom. The lavender bush is bare of flowers, solely a bush of foliage, and I am surprised. Surprised at the color. Where in my mind lavender is always a solid, sturdy purple, the leaves here are a distinct silvery green. This massive plant, one I have always considered to be strong in color and scent, pales. I am not disappointed, merely amazed at how different one's idea of something can be from the reality.

I decide to research what exactly it is about lavender that

makes it so calming for the mind, makes me feel so at peace in my body. I find myself bored by the science, or at least unimpressed. There is something essential lost while trying to prove what I know innately. Lavender calms me—what is the value in questioning this, in trying to understand how or why?

I learn one interesting fact in my research, that the molecule in lavender that triggers the relaxation response is called linalool. I learn that this molecule exists in basil, too, which makes sense to me, though I cannot explain why. I just know that playing with either feels like peace.

Venice, a city on the water (is this the antithesis to the city on a hill?), floods easily. While there, I experience one particularly bad instance of *acqua alta* (high water), where the water rises above ground level and floods everything. In a matter of moments, everyone outside is suddenly clothed in knee high rain boots. Though it is my first *acqua alta*, it is certainly a well-honed routine for the people here, who begin various processes to remove water from inside their homes and stores. I borrow the mother's pair of boots and go out to explore, filming everything I see. I am stunned, watching the waves crash over the sidewalks and into shops and houses. There is water everywhere, small puddles of it further inland, and shin high closer to the canals. The sidewalks and walkways have disappeared, covered in the tide. It is hard not to laugh a little. For all human ingenuity, here we all are, wading in the water, all floating on this remarkable drowning city.

This flooding takes a toll on the plant life of Venice, the father I live with explains to me. He points out one of the trees in the yard and tells me that it is struggling due to an over-absorption of saltwater. When the lagoon floods, the water from the canal seeps through the lawn and is absorbed via the roots of the tree. Now, after all I have learned, I understand that this buildup of salt can ultimately kill a plant. I wonder if the tree there, *a Venezia*, is still alive, or if it has succumbed to the flow of the water around it.

Each day as I walk from the little house to the main house,

or from the main house to outside, I pass by the large lavender bush. Every time I walk by, a phantom whiff of lavender enters my nose. I have never been certain if the foliage of lavender is fragrant too, or if it is just the flowers. And I don't care what any expert has to say on the matter (I would rather live in the mystery of it). I question this because sometimes when I am far away, I will smell the strongest lavender scent pouring off just the foliage. *Of course the leaves have fragrance*, I will note in these moments.

Other times, I will rub the leaves myself and shove my whole face in them, and there will be nothing, not even a hint of that sweet smell. I do not know what this means. Perhaps it simply means I am hopeful that the beauty of lavender can exist year-round, rather than the few weeks it is in bloom. Perhaps it means hope is enough to trick the mind into creating a scent that is not actually there.

Each day I pass by the lavender bush and each day I settle into my life in Venice more and more. I am still sad, I am still mourning, but I am also falling in love with another Italian city—my favorite hobby. I spend as much time on the water as I can, letting it feed me, carry me. This is an easy feat when all public transportation takes the form of boats. I am constantly floating, en route and in my mind.

I start to think I can stay in Venice indefinitely, and the family seems happy to have me. I have begun carving out a little space for myself. My language skills are improving, my sense of belonging increasing. Everything is starting to feel okay, a little better. I am mourning, and at the same time I know I will be okay.

And then Papa John dies.

Papa John is Dede's husband, her third to be precise. They have been together for as long as I have been alive. Papa John was always my grandpa, always a presence in my life. Their wedding remains the only one I have ever been in—myself, my sister, and Papa John's biological granddaughter all walked down the aisle as flower girls.

There is something so beautiful to me about the fact that Dede and Papa John got together later in life. They had both already had children, had already reached the high points in their careers, had settled comfortably into retirement. When I asked Dede how they met, she regaled me with a tale of courtship and romance. *I had several gentlemen callers, but Papa John was the most persistent!* Thank goodness for that.

They were together for the last twenty-four years of their respective lives. On paper, two people could not be more different, but in person, it worked. Being in their presence, thinking of them, knowing a love like theirs existed, all this was a reminder to me that love is not sensical. It is feeling. It is embodied. It is universal and gorgeous and something beyond words. Nothing but nothing can be prioritized above love. Nothing but nothing makes love impossible. Love, true love, transcends human banality.

I find out Papa John dies when my mom calls me, six in the morning her time, noon for me. I am in the midst of an Italian class when she calls and I cannot answer, and yet I already know in my bones exactly what she will later say. Papa John had gotten sick soon after Dede died, and the second I see my mom's name on my phone, I know his illness has gotten the best of him.

I am devastated, and I am calmed. Papa John loved Dede more than life itself. I cannot imagine that—loving like that, losing like that. I am sad for me that he is gone, and I am grateful for him that he is. Grateful that he is no longer alone, no longer aching, no longer without his blushing bride.

I stand outside by the lavender bush, and I cry. I cry because I am in a beautiful place, and I am all alone. I cry because I am tired of crying and tired of hurting. I cry because I came to Italy looking for peace and family and a sense of belonging. I cry because I have found all these things and they are not enough, and they are not quite my own, and I know in my gut what I need and what I am not giving to myself.

And so, I decide to go home. Home. Home is a loaded word.

What is a home?

A home for a lavender plant is easy to describe. We can talk about its original home, trace it back to its earliest known origins, to the expanses of Southern France and the sandy Mediterranean coasts. Or we can examine this exact plant, its current home. The home of a lavender is where it becomes established, where it develops its roots. It takes a while for plants to establish themselves. First the soil must be dug up and loosened. Compost can be added in, and the soil amended depending on the needs of the variety. The plant is placed into the hole, and the roots are covered with soil. Then both plant and caretaker get to work—the plant begins spreading its roots out, reaching into and exploring its environment. The caretaker must water and regularly check in on the progress of the plant, ensuring that it is settling into its new home. Eventually the lavender will stretch its roots out, searching for water and nutrients. It is through this process of searching that it becomes established, fully rooted into the soil. It is through this process of searching that it finds its home.

A simple way to test if a plant is rooted is to give a gentle tug. If you feel the plant pull up easily, it still has a way to go in getting settled. However, if you give a little tug and you feel resistance, feel the soil pulling back against you—you'll know your plant has found its way home.

This is what Papa John's death does to me. It gives me a little tug.

I want so badly to root myself in Italy. I want to take my past and put it in a drawer, put it away on a high shelf—out of sight, out of mind. I want to shove the past away and I want to fly across a whole ocean, and I want to speak a completely different language, both literally and figuratively. I want to establish myself, want to find a home, want to create a family, want to build a life in this place. And then.

This hand, this hand that we can call the universe or God or my own inner voice (and really, I believe those three things to be one and the same), this hand gives me a little tug. It says: *Hey, your grandma is dead and now your grandpa is too. Is that enough to pull you out? Is that enough to shake you? Are your roots long enough, strong enough, to withstand this? To not question if this is the right soil for you?*

This hand tugs and I fly up and out with ease. Before I know it, I am on a plane, flying from Venice to New York. Returning to my childhood home in Connecticut.

I return home because I know there is still work to be done. After Dede's passing, in the couple of weeks before I moved to Italy, I felt something shift. Between myself and my parents, myself and my environment. Dede's death brought something into focus, but I was not willing to look yet, and instead headed onward to Florence, to Venice. This shift becomes impossible to ignore after Papa John's death, and it's like it's not even a choice: I must go home. Must take the past down off the shelf I hid it on. Examine it. Hold it. Let it go instead of ignoring it and hoping it disappears on its own. Even death requires attention. Even that which has faded must be acknowledged in order to bury it, in order to truly move on.

At home I continue to mourn and flail. I wonder if I was wrong, wrong to leave Italy, wrong to come home. I worry that I am absurd for making all my decisions from a place of heart rather than one of pragmatism. I do not know what I am going to do for work, I do not know what the future holds, not at all. I feel like a moron for not sticking to my plan (of staying in Italy, of learning Italian, of creating a life there). What am I doing? I find discomfort in the unknown. I am nothing if not exactly like every other human I know.

I purchase lavender seeds one day, because I can and because I am bored and because I decide it might feel good to grow something, might be a nice way to pass the time. I ignore the warnings I find online about how challenging it can be to grow lavender from seed. I find a shallow plastic tub, the kind of container takeout food comes in. I fill the container with two inches of potting soil, tuck the small seeds in, and mist the fresh earth with a spray bottle.

I find a suggestion online to buy a special heating mat to place underneath the container to stimulate growth. The warmth of the mat is supposed to mimic the warming soil of spring. I do not wish to spend the money and naïvely assume that the seeds will sprout anyway, that the bright south-facing window I have put them in will provide enough heat. Later I will learn that an easy way to provide warmth to soil is by watering with lukewarm water. Simple solutions are so beautiful in their obviousness.

I attempt to grow lavender from seed, and I fail. The seeds never sprout. They feel a lot like me. Shoved into some dirt without care or consideration, trying to make a home in inhospitable lands. I am flailing and I am lost and I do not know what I am doing. Home does not feel right, no matter where I want that home to be.

I try to figure out what matters to me, what I want to do with my life, how I want to spend my time. And—as you may have already guessed, reading this—the answer is resoundingly: plants. I realize I want to spend my time playing with these sweet alive things, learning more, understanding, nurturing.

Over the next few weeks, I visit the garden center near my house. My childhood home is situated in the ideal spot for any nature lover. Directly across the street from us there are no homes. Instead, there is a forest and a pond—a gorgeous protected open space home to a variety of woodland creatures. This open space extends down the road. If one walks along and through the open space long enough, they will stumble upon a garden center. It is here that I find myself visiting on multiple occasions. I just want to be with the quiet alive things.

It is a beautiful place, full of flowers and plants of every imaginable kind. I visit a few times with my mom, purchasing new pots for the aloe plants I have at home and finding daffodils and violas for my mom to plant at our front door. One day, while my mom is at work, I decide to visit the garden center on my own. In our backyard, we have a gorgeous white hydrangea tree. A group of her friends gifted it to her last year after Dede died. My mom keeps talking about how lovely it would be to have something planted around the hydrangea. Something low to the ground to complement it. To hold it.

I decide that I will surprise her by planting something beautiful underneath it that she can come home to—a garden that appears without effort must be healing, I hope. I know nothing, very little, about plants, though I am desperate to learn. I know that I want to grow something that, like the hydrangea tree, will last for years to come. I walk over to the garden center and begin to explore.

I look through the pretty annual flowers, and though they excite me, I know they will only last for a season. I want something with staying power. I peruse the perennials, but nothing grabs me. Finally, I explore the herbs. Mint, thyme, rosemary, several sages, all lined up in neat rows. At the very end of the collection, I have my answer. Lavender.

I do not know it then, will not know it until months later, but this one moment changes the trajectory of my life. This one moment is one of those moments (like every moment) where everything hinges, where everything shifts. I ask my coworker some months later: *How did I get the job at the garden center? Why did you guys hire me?* And she tells me: *You came in by yourself and were looking at the lavender, and something about that made me think you should work here.* That simple.

This is where I have been since. Working at the garden center and growing things here and working in my own backyard and growing things there. A year of growing, giving, green things.

All spring and summer I watch the lavender with a keen eye. It is my first project in the garden, my first attempt as a caretaker of the natural world, and I want it to be perfect, want the plants to grow huge and strong. I plant them in a circle around the hydrangea tree.

Soon after planting, I realize I have done absolutely everything wrong. I am a perfectionist, and I need everything to be, well, perfect. The lavenders teach me the first lesson of plants: that they are alive and that they have needs—like any living entity. I took this for granted before, the alive-ness of plants.

I am getting ahead of myself. I plant the lavender plants (ten in all) around the hydrangea. The variety is called grosso lavender, apparently a very hardy and prolific bloomer. Seems perfect. I plant them in a circle, and they are perfect, and then I begin to research. I ask the internet: what does full sun mean? (I see this phrase used on the tags that come with the plants. It does not occur to me, of course, to find out what this means before I begin planting). Full sun, I learn, means six or more hours of sun exposure daily. The spot where I have planted the lavender gets four hours, maybe five. Strike one. Next, I become curious as to how large the plants will be at full size. I learn that they can reach two to three feet at maturity. I have planted my lavenders much closer together than that. Strike two.

I decide to move the plants. I shift them to the other side of the yard. My original plan, of having them surround the tree, is forsaken. Instead, all I care about is finding the proper home for my lavender. A sunny spot with well-draining soil, nicely distanced apart with room for them to spread and grow. I find a nice open space in one of the beds of soil and plant them. I even get out a tape measure this time, carefully measuring three feet of space between each plant, so as not to crowd them out.

My lavender becomes a barometer of my gardening skills. On days when the lavender looks happy and healthy, I am allowed to be proud of my efforts. On days when I spy dead leaves or soggy seeming soil, I am filled with shame. How am I supposed to make a career out of this, how can I claim to know anything at all about plants when I cannot properly care for these sweet lavenders? These plants that gave me my job, gave me direction, gave me purpose?

Over time I must come to terms with the fact that my lavender is struggling, my lavender is suffering, my lavender is not okay. The spot I have chosen, though sunnier than by the hydrangea tree, is still a bit too shaded to mimic the hot all-day sun that lavender traditionally thrives under. I keep willing the plants to grow, willing them to bloom, but without the heat and energy a full day's sun provides, they do not have the strength to create. I am heartbroken. I feel like a failure. I leave them be, unsure of how to proceed, knowing they are unhappy where they are. Knowing that my attempt to make our garden more beautiful was in vain.

One night I am lying in bed trying to fall asleep and I am anxious, so anxious. The kind of anxiety where I can feel my heart beating so hard I can feel it against the bone, and though I know logically my heart can't actually beat out of my chest, it feels that way—like it might just. I can feel the whole cavity of my abdomen, I can feel every inch of my body, but not in a good way, not in a present way. It's in a way that's too much, all at once, painful. Presence isn't painful. It just is. This isn't.

This is that kind of anxiety, and I don't know what to do. But then I read my own words, the first paragraph of this essay, and I am reminded. Reminded of how lavender can calm. I grab my little rollerball full of lavender oil, and I press my head back into my pillow and I rub oil. I rub it all over my neck and my wrists and slather it under my nostrils. I rub it all over my face, all over my arms. I want to bathe in the lavender, I want to live in it, I want to become it. I know that it can calm me, and so it *has* to, I am begging it to. And it does.

There is power in the distilled form of lavender only because of the human hand, the human desire to harness the plant and carry it with us always. We took this plant, this flower that smells so beautiful, and we said—let me get to the essence of that, let me enhance it, let me bottle this up so that it may do good. Whoever did this first, I am grateful.

Lavender, the flower itself, smells stronger if you rub it between your fingers, crushing and releasing the scent molecules.

Breathe in. Breathe out.

I take my rollerball out of my nightstand now, and layer a bit on my neck, just one swipe on each side. I breathe in and out. In and out. Always longer out than in. If you breathe in longer than you breathe out, you can hyperventilate. If you breathe out longer than you breathe in, however, you can calm your whole body. I forget the science behind this, but it's there and it holds. Three seconds in, hold, seven out. Just like lavender, it has yet to fail me. In, out. I calm, I feel my body relax. Lavender reminds me that the essence of something is not the same as the source. Lavender reminds me that this might not actually matter.

I decide that the lavender in my yard should not stay there. It does not belong there, despite how desperately I want it to. I want it to bloom for me. I want to have a constant and personal source of my favorite scent. I feel like a petulant child, until I decide: it is time to let go. It is time to stop trying to force lavender to flourish where it cannot. It is time to stop asking the Earth to bend her rules for me.

I pull the lavender out of the ground, once again. I am surprised upon doing so to discover just how well-rooted the plants have become, despite their sad looking foliage. I compost the plants, thank them for what they have taught me, thank them for trying at all. I plant three white Japanese anemones in their place—plants that are more accustomed to the lighting conditions, plants that can actually thrive. Had I known then what I know now, would I have planted the lavender still? Is it wrong if I say yes?

I save one of the lavender plants in a pot, moving it to the absolute sunniest location my yard can provide. There it sits still now, almost winter. It is not thriving, exactly, but it is not dying. It just is. It is just, being. It may never bloom, might not even grow, but I am giving it a chance to settle in. I am keeping just a little bit of hope alive, for old times' sake.

I think home has little to do with logic and a lot to do with feeling. We cannot necessarily know if home is right or wrong until we plant ourselves in a place and see how our feet feel, see if we root ourselves out or flounder.

I went searching for a home in Italy, a family there. My body knew what my brain did not. My body said: you already have a home, and that home may be messy and frustrating and scary and full of pain and decades of resentment—all these things may be true—but that does not change the fact that that place, that home, is still yours. My body said: there is still healing to be done with your family. There is still healing that can happen at home.

I am thankful that I listened to my body, that I let myself be uprooted out of Italy. That my roots there were shallow enough to leave, to lift out with ease. Coming home has been the greatest gift I could give myself. It has given me the opportunity to mend the relationships with my parents, to mend the relationships with my home itself, and—perhaps most magically—to learn to care for the Earth, to tend to the very land my home lives upon.

Had I not come home I would never have gotten my job at the garden center, and I never would have learned all the lessons I've learned, and I never would have decided to write this essay, nor this book. Home—the feeling of it, the comfort of it—has brought everything together. Home is not about a place, but a feeling. The lavender cannot put into words, cannot articulate, why it blooms best where it does. And yet, it is written into the DNA of the plant exactly how much light it needs, exactly the kind of soil it will thrive in, what nutrients will make it prosper and which will overload it. The lavender finds home through its roots, through its feet, through feeling its way through the soil and determining if it's a proper match.

I like to think I have learned to discover home in the same way. I think it's the same way Dede knew her home too, could feel Russia in her bones while living in Connecticut. Because to love a place is one thing, but to live in it is another, and though her heart loved Russia so deeply, her feet sought to stand on ground that was close to her children, her grandchildren. Her body held her home near those she loved.

I wanted to make lavender grow where it could not. Maybe that was selfish of me, but I like to think it was just me being hopeful, me loving deeply. Loving places. Loving being here in my own backyard, and simultaneously trying to carry a little piece of the Mediterranean, of Italy, home with me. Melding all the homes I know and love into one.

Everything happens exactly as it needs to. And plants are there to witness it all, guide us through it all. I wanted to grow lavender in my yard so it could be utilitarian, useful. Healing me always. I thought the only value lavender had was in the feeling it could provide me with. But lavender is always doing, so much and without asking. It has taught me. Taught me what it means to be home. What it means to find soil that suits you. Lavender is a teacher and a witness. It watched me begin my healing process in Arizona. It held me and carried me over the last few years in all its many forms. It saw me mourn in Venice, and it has been here while I heal at home. It was present through it all, even when I neglected its needs or resented the same. It is wiser than me, and for knowing it I know—I am trying to understand—that which I still have to learn. That which the plants still have to teach me.

I am trying to trace back to a time before plants colored my life, but I cannot. They were always there, have always been here, silent, ever-present. Waiting for me to notice. To pay attention to them. *Aspetta*, I say. Wait. Just a little longer. I'm on my way. I'm on my way.

Aloe Vera

IT was Dede who first instilled in me a love of plants. I did not see it then, while it was happening, but I can trace it back now, can see with clear eyes that it was she who first taught me the truth of these chlorophyll-full creatures, showed me all the wonders of the natural world. In my youth she handed me a seed of love, of knowledge, one that lay dormant for years. After she is gone, that seed bursts forth, a bloom of admiration for the green things of this world.

It all began with aloe. For as long as I can remember, Dede kept an aloe vera plant in her apartment. Dede, mind you, was the definition of an aesthetically minded person. The way she clothed her body, the way she filled her spaces, everything was done with taste and consideration and an innate understanding of beauty, of style. She loved soft fabrics, she loved luxury, she loved cultivating a sense of wonder. This was her greatest talent: making her corner of the world more beautiful for herself, and for everyone around her.

Her apartment was full of visually pleasing objects—works of art adorning deep blue walls, impressive and stoic sculptures tucked into the corners between elegant yet comfortable sofas and chairs, lush carpeting, and perfectly selected furniture to complement the space. The aloe that she kept in her apartment, in my eyes, did not fit.

Aloe is spiky, ranging from light to dark green, with serrated edges. It grows in a rosette formation, with sharp thick leaves that jut upward and encircle each other. It is a desert plant, a survivor. It is not, in my loving opinion, aesthetically pleasing. And yet Dede, the woman with more taste and an eye for design than anyone I know, kept a large planter full of it at all times.

In the warm summer months it lived out on the balcony, to soak up as much sunlight as it could, and during the rest of the year it lived inside. Wherever it was, it was ever-present, a constant fixture in her home, as enduring and intriguing as Dede herself. It has taken me the gift of hindsight to finally understand its purpose, its place.

As I write right now, I close my eyes and try to meditate on aloe. I let the images flow. Meditation can be whatever we want it to be. I always laugh, lovingly, when people say they aren't good at meditation, or they don't know how. Meditation, mindfulness, presence, we're all doing it, all the time. A therapist once told me that to practice mindfulness is to pay attention on purpose. But I think it's just to pay attention. I think we are always, here. Always, now. Always, being. And so, to meditate is the natural state. Sometimes we just do it with more awareness. I don't have a word for that. I don't know if this makes sense, if it matters. I'm writing it down regardless.

I am trying to meditate on aloe. Which means I read what I have written thus far, and I bring the image of my aloe plant to mind, and I see what flows. When I refer to my aloe plant, it is the largest and oldest of my collection that comes to mind, though I possess several. Possess. I live with. I care for. To possess seems crude—can't quite capture what I feel. And is it even accurate to say that I care for it? It cares for me.

I bring the image of this plant to mind, my eldest aloe—maybe six years old at this point, purchased online on a whim one day. I didn't know then why I bought it, and I can't say with certainty now. All I know is it's here, with me, and perhaps that means it was meant to be here. Perhaps things happen exactly as they should, without our understanding or even choice. Perhaps the aloe is here because it was always going to be here. Always needed to be here, when I needed it most.

I meditate on the image of this plant that is meant to be here and I am avoiding saying, avoiding describing, what arises. The image that pops into my mind is of the day my dog died this spring. Barclay, a beautiful westie, passed away suddenly at age fourteen in April. When he dies, I cry more than I cried after my grandma died, more than after my grandpa died, more than I cried after a friend of mine died years ago (which I have long thought was my crying limit). I cry until there are no more tears. It is a loss I cannot grasp, because I did not expect it to feel like loss.

Animals are a lot like plants in that they understand existence more innately, more simply, than humans do. I think we complicate our existence by thinking. I'm doing it right now. Spinning myself in circles, weaving a web of thought, when the simplest, easiest, most natural thing is to just be. To breathe. Animals and plants do not worry about the past, the future. They are always here, present, in the moment. And yet I cannot help but wonder if Barclay feared death, if he understood he was dying. I wonder if plants do, too.

After he dies, I don't know where to place my body. I don't know where to place the loss in my body. It feels stupid and immature to be so upset over a dog. And yet I am, and to judge those feelings feels equally immature. I am a mess. I am ridiculous. I don't know what to do.

And so, I do the only thing I know how, and return to life, return to the healing growing living entity in my home. My aloe. I walk into the hallway that connects the house to the garage. Full of windows on either side, it has become the perfect home for my collection of aloes. The mother plant, impressive and huge, surrounded by her babies of varying sizes, all in their own pots. I sit next to them, and I weep. I am held.

I stroke the leaves of the plants. I feel the spikes that line either side of each leaf. I sit with them. I have my knees pulled up to my chest, my face and eyes tender from tears, and I sit. I have lost one living thing this day, I have lost so much life from my life this year, and yet here, all around me, are these beautiful alive things. These silent creatures, who hold me without arms and nurture me without thought. And suddenly I understand—aesthetic is not the only form of beauty. Healing is beauty too.

After Barclay dies, I take it upon myself to call the vet. My mom is distraught, and I want to do something, want to feel useful. The receptionist who answers offers her condolences, explains our options. We decide as a family that cremation is the best choice—we are afraid of burying him in the yard, in case another animal digs him up for a meal. It's funny to have to consider these things. How do we outwit life? How do we outwit the hunger of a creature in order to protect the decaying body of another? We burn the one we love.

My parents eventually take Barclay away. He leaves our home in comfort, in death. My dad, still teary-eyed, carries him out in his plushy bed. We just want him to be at peace.

My parents leave with Barclay, and I return to the aloes. I continue to sit with them, to mourn with them. They speak to me, though we do not share a common tongue. They hold me. *We're still here*, they say. *We aren't going anywhere, not today.* Sometimes, even in the face of loss, knowing plants exist at all is enough to comfort me.

My love of aloe feels hard to quantify. How do you explain a love of magic? It feels so obvious, so *of course*. Aloe has my heart. Could it be any other way?

Most people are familiar with aloe in some capacity. It is the ultimate and most tried and true solution for sunburn. Any supermarket, drug store, or the like will have a shelf of aloe products, designed for soothing and healing burns. While the powers of aloe are potent in any form, there is nothing quite like getting it fresh from the leaf.

The power of aloe comes from the juice, the liquid that lives inside the leaves. This juice is so healing because it is mostly water—is life—combined with a remarkable mix of nutrients. These are the nutrients that sustain the plant, and when applied to skin, they can work wonders, healing and soothing and calming many ails.

When I was a child, I would often spend time at Dede's apartment. Dede was not a typical grandmother (first and foremost because she chose to be called Dede, as opposed to grandma). She was eccentric, creative, gorgeous, slightly wild, with a voice and accent so indeterminate it was certainly just her own. But not put on, not contrived, just, Dede. Perfectly her.

Visiting Dede at her apartment was a bit like visiting the Queen mixed with visiting Disneyland. There was always a sense of formality in the air and simultaneously such wonder, such magic, endless possibility.

On one such occasion we spent the day lounging by the pool. One of the highlights of visiting Dede was the pool at her apartment complex, a child's heaven. I, ever obstinate, was never the best about applying and reapplying sunscreen, and on this day my nose got a nasty burn.

Dede, once we returned upstairs, immediately got to work. She grabbed a sharp knife from the kitchen, headed to the balcony where the aloe sat, and sliced a chunk off one of the leaves. I watched her carefully slice the leaf lengthwise, and then, before I knew what was happening, she was slathering the goop on my nose and then all over my little face. I was disgusted and simultaneously soothed. The aloe provided an immediate cooling and calming effect, and the tinge of the sunburn began to fade. The next morning, there was no burn in sight.

I miss her dearly. I am filled with longing for her to soothe me once more. I am saddened that I did not understand then, could not understand, all the ways she loved me. All the times she healed me, without me ever having to ask. All the times I should have said thank you and did not. Thank you. I love you. This is all for you.

My mom has a Dede aloe story, too, one that I ask her to regale me with once again so that I may write it down. It goes something like this: Dede and my mom were taking a hat-making class, some fun adult education program they had found. At the class, they were using hot glue guns and my mom scorched herself on the metal of the tool. Dede, ever wise, suggested that my mom stop in at her apartment for some aloe on the way home. At first my mom refused, but as the pain increased, she agreed.

When they arrived at Dede's, the same routine ensued. She took out a knife, cut off a leaf, and sliced it open, revealing the transformative liquid inside. This time, instead of just rubbing some of the juice on the burn like she did with me, she took a whole half of the leaf and placed it down with the juice touching my mom's skin. She wrapped the whole thing up in a bandage. My mom described being perplexed, seemed as disgusted as I first had been by the gloppy mess. But then the next morning she took the bandage off, and there was nothing there. No blister, no burn, no mark whatsoever. Aloe had turned back time, taken away the pain, with such tender ease.

I do this now, with my own aloes. Whenever I or anyone else gets burned, I go through the same process that my grandmother did. One that she did not explicitly teach me, not with words, but through repeated action and observation. I go to my largest aloe, the most mature, and slice off the outermost leaf. Sometimes I take the whole leaf straight from the base, other times just a little bit. It depends on need. It depends on what I feel the plant can give, what I am willing to take.

Last summer I watched as the mother plant shrank, as I took leaf after leaf to heal the ones I love. She shrank and she kept giving, putting out baby plants around herself. Constantly growing, constantly doing for everyone, everything around her.

It makes sense that the large mature plant is called the mother. The one who gives without asking, who will sacrifice herself to nurture the babies (the pups, as they're called) that she creates. Mother is creation, mother is life. But mother needs healing, too.

I have to stop taking so much from the mother plant. Have to let her be. I remove the baby plants from her pot, repotting them on their own, so she does not have to nurture so much, does not have to give of herself. I add fertilizer to her soil to fortify her, and then just let her be. She deserves to be. To be cared for.

At the end of Dede's life, I watched this same shift occur. The mother, the matriarch, who had given so much of herself to her offspring, it was now her time to be cared for, nurtured. I admire my mom and my aunt, who for years took care of every facet of Dede's life. They took her to doctor's appointments, dealt with her finances, made sure she always had everything she needed. Mothers need our care too. Sometimes most of all.

My largest aloe, my mother plant, will not live forever, though I'm hopeful she has at least a good five or six years left in her. I wonder how many more pups she will create in the meantime. I wonder how many more humans she will heal.

I take my aloes outside in the summertime now, just like Dede once did. I want to let them feel the sun hit their leaves directly, without the barrier of a windowpane in the way. There's nothing quite like that: sun on skin, bathing in the warm glow of the entity that provides for us all, is the source of all life.

Aloes are the beginning of my plant story, the origin. The first aloe I get, the one that still sits in my home now, survives only because aloes do best with a bit of benign neglect. Native to desert environments, aloes thrive when their care in a home setting mimics this, that desert feel. They want dry, sandy soil, minimal fertilizing, and as much sunlight as possible. The plant does well for the first few years because I have nothing to give it, no mothering in me, and that is enough.

Aloes are resilient. They are very hard to kill. I like to think that I am like that, too—that the aloes and I have something in common there. I can withstand a lot. I should not have to. Nor should they. Even the tough creatures of this world deserve tenderness.

Now I am more tender with my aloes. I care for myself these days, beautifully so, and thus I have the energy to care for those I love. I tend to my needs, and in doing so I give myself the space and time and energy to care for my precious aloes, who have cared for me ten-fold.

I am sitting here now with two of my aloes. These are my two smallest. I move them into the living room at summer's end because this is the room with the best lighting (south-facing windows), and I want them to have everything they need. I sit here now and glance at them every few moments. I am trying to translate for the plants on these pages, and I know I am failing, know I cannot quite grasp what they're saying. *Tell me*, I beg, *tell me what you mean.*

It's like they smile at me. *We're just here*, they declare. *We're just here, soaking up the sun and making the air cleaner for you and growing, bit by bit. We just exist. What more can we say?*

These two little aloes started turning brown a few weeks ago, seemingly out of nowhere. They are getting less sun than when they were outside, and so it doesn't make sense that they should start to brown now. It doesn't make sense, and yet—like so much of life—it is happening anyways. I feel helpless, feel like a failure. These creatures, so small, rely on me, just as I one day will rely on them to heal me. Right now, it is my turn. I take a chance and dilute a very minuscule portion of fertilizer in water and feed them with it. My instincts turn out to be correct, and the little boost of nutrients is enough to help them heal themselves. Within twenty-four hours their brown leaves begin morphing back to green.

I am so proud of myself, and so proud of them. I point out the change to my mother (who first noted the browning weeks ago). I exclaim to her, *I'm a magician!*

No, she corrects. *You're a gardener.*

I am sitting with these two aloes, now a happy vibrant green, and I want to cry—happy tears. My gratitude for these plants feels immeasurable, my love for them infinite. These pups, these babies from the mother, are so small, so precious, and I am honored to be their caretaker. It feels divine, feels like a gift from the Earth, sent to strengthen my spirit.

When I care for the aloes, when I help them to grow, they

care for me in return. We are in a constant state of symbiosis, the aloes and I. We are united in our cause. We are healers, and we understand: the healing of oneself is the healing of the whole world. The healing of one plant is the healing of my own body. To care for oneself is to care for those you love, because to care for oneself allows oneself to be the fullest and most generous one can be. The care of others, of plants and people and animals, allows that care to come back. To love is to love is to love. Let us love and care for ourselves, let us love and care for others, let us prioritize nothing above the understanding that we are one, and that love and nurturing can heal us all.

Everything we need is here. We have been gifted an Earth that is so bountiful, so precious and gorgeous. Aloe is a reminder of this. Aloe feels like pure magic, like something that should not exist. You can grow something in your home that can heal you, physically and rapidly and so smoothly. Our bodies work with plants, need plants, rely on them. They are intrinsic to our existence, intrinsic to our healing.

Aloe is so healing and magical and perfect and good that it feels like it should not exist, and yet it does, and of course it does. We are not at odds with this perfect planet we find ourselves on. We are one with it, intrinsically a part of it, and of course everything we could ever need is right here, right at our fingertips. All the natural world asks of us in exchange for all that it gives is that we return the favor. That we mother our mother when she needs it.

When my grandmother becomes ill, it is not a question that my mom and aunt step in, step up. They say, with every action, every moment of care: it is now time to nurture the woman who nurtured us. It is our turn to give back to she who has given.

Mother Earth is suffering, tremendously. We have taken and taken all she can give. She has given ceaselessly, and now must be replenished, must be fortified with tender care. It is our turn to return the favor of love, of nurturing. It is our turn.

Aloe shows me daily, reminds me: the plants have given me

so much. The plants have healed me since childhood and will continue to heal me. The plants will never stop healing, will never stop cleansing our air and oceans, will never stop producing food for creatures big and small. They will never stop giving. It is just what they do.

Let me be like the plants. Let us all. It is time to give back. It is time to say, I am the aloe now. I am so magic and healing I should not exist. And yet, of course I do. We must act, must do, must be a part of the cycle. It is the natural way. It is integral to our survival, our species, our planet to understand: mother needs nurturing too.

Where will we be when our first mother needs us? What can we give to an Earth who has given us everything?

I will be here. I can give my all.

Pruning

I AM GIFTED my job at the garden center by the universe. I tell the universe one day (I tell myself, a piece of the universe) that I don't know what I'm doing, but I know I love plants. *Give me something to do with plants*, I beg, *anything at all*.

The universe appears in myriad forms. She is always listening, always ready to help us along on our journey when we ask for it. I call out: let me be with the green things of this world. Bonnie, owner of the garden center near my home, heeds this call. People show me every day that the universe is always listening. All we must do is speak.

The best training for plants is to begin, and I learn this where we start: at the beginning. I arrive for work during the busy season. It's why I am hired in the first place—May is hectic for a nursery, and they need an extra set of hands. *I have hands*, I say. *Let them be needed*.

I arrive the first day at my new job expecting to receive some level of training, some shadowing of more senior staff members. I expect this especially because Bonnie knows how little I know about plants, that I have absolutely zero professional experience with these living critters. She hires me anyway, because, as she says, *you love plants*. I wonder if it's that plastered on my face, in my body, in my bones. I do, I do. I love them so.

Bonnie gives me a brief tour of the facilities, showing me the different greenhouses and buildings, telling me their various nicknames—names that will take me the entirety of my tenure to fully ingrain. Top house, head house, second greenhouse (which is sometimes just "next door"), hoop house, weed mat, bench mart. I nod along at the quick succession, certain I will forget it all. She shows me the plants, indoors and out, and then it is time to begin.

For my first task, Bonnie puts me to work in the bench mart, a small greenhouse-like structure set up outside that houses all of the herbs and some lettuces and vegetables. She gives me a pair of shears ("snips"), shows me the mint, and tasks me with cutting it back. Tour over, training complete, in the course of several minutes. This flusters me, but I will soon discover it is the best way to learn. You can talk about plants, study them for as long as you please, but the real lessons only start when we get our hands dirty.

I am immediately soothed by the fragrance of the mint, though simultaneously stressed at the task of cutting it back. Bonnie explains that clipping the mint back encourages it to grow bushier, fuller, as opposed to lanky and long. This is my introduction to pruning.

Pruning encompasses a wide range of gardening techniques. Generally, pruning speaks to cutting away parts of the plant. Sometimes we do this when leaves of the plant have died, either from over or under watering, or simply as part of the natural process of the plant, shedding the old in favor of new growth. We remove these dead or dying bits to improve the appearance of the plant and so that it does not waste energy holding onto old leaves. That energy can be returned to the plant for growth and production.

Some pruning looks like what Bonnie has me do with the mint on the first day—cutting the plant back to encourage bushiness, fullness. When we snip a healthy plant back, cut off some of its still growing tips, it encourages the plant to branch out where it is cut and to grow new branches from the base. Instead of continuing to grow the way it was, in one line, pruning these plants creates a fork in the road.

Pruning can also be used to shape a plant more intricately, the way a bonsai tree is carefully created. With each snip of leaves and branches, we craft the direction the plant will take—to an extent. We can try to encourage the direction and movement that we want, but ultimately, the plant itself is always running the show.

I find pruning, in its varied forms, incredibly relaxing. A meditation. A cleanse. It becomes my favorite activity at work, and I seek it out when possible.

I find particular pleasure in deadheading, the task of removing spent blooms from a plant in order to allow energy for new ones to form. There is such beauty, such simplicity, in clearing away that which has died in order to make space for new growth.

Petunias become my favorite flowers to prune. At work we have petunias of every imaginable color, lined up on multiple benches. They are sun-loving plants, desiring at least six hours of direct sunshine a day. Most of the petunias live on a long bench in the center of the pavement. All along the grassy edges of the property stand a mass of trees, which cast their shade all around them. This is of benefit to the shade-loving plants we keep near the fence, but the petunias must be kept out in the middle, away from the dappled light the leafy behemoths produce.

I work methodically when it comes time for petunia pruning, working my way from one end of the bench to the other, plant by plant. After a heavy rain, when the delicate petunias become sad and mushy, the deadheading process can take several hours, especially when factoring in the constant stream of customers for whom I must pause my work to assist. I clear the muck off the petunias and deposit everything into a compost bin as I go.

Other times, the petunias are less in need of deadheading and instead have become overgrown and lanky. On these occasions, I use snips or my fingernails, when they are sharp enough, and pluck a few inches of growth off the ends of the plants. This encourages the stems to branch out and produce new growth from the base, creating a fuller, more plentiful appearance. More beauty for the human eye, more food for the bees and butterflies.

The reason I find the pruning of petunias so gratifying is that the results are almost immediate, or as immediate as anything can be in the plant world. One day, Bonnie points me in the direction of the petunia flats. The main bench of petunias contains four-inch plastic pots. The flats are tucked away on a different bench and contain six-packs of individual petunia plugs—much smaller and less established than their four-inch counterparts.

We attend to the flats less than the larger pots, because they are smaller, less expensive, and more out of sight than the main bench of petunias. Since they have been neglected a bit already, a particularly heavy rain leaves them looking, in a word, atrocious. I begin.

The petunia flats are in desperate need of both deadheading and pinching back. Covered in gross, rain-soaked petals, and laughably leggy, the flats appear at first to be an overwhelming task. I work on each six-pack individually, holding it in my left hand and using my right to clean. I pluck away all the rain-soaked flowers. Then, I evaluate. I leave the shorter stems alone, but when I find an overgrown section, I am brutal. I chop off chunks of petunia liberally, watch the loose bits cascade into the compost bin. I do this over and over again, until each of the petunia flats have been cleaned.

When I complete this process, the petunias look, admittedly, quite sad. Few flowers remain, just small clumps of green leaves. A few days later, however, the scene is transformed. Pools of pink, purple, red, and white petunias appear before my eyes. Bees and butterflies once more enjoy the sweet nectar they provide. Where before the pruning process there was a mess of bedraggled flowers and barren stems, now rows of lush-looking leaves and petals stand at attention, ready to be taken home by customers so they can create beauty of their own.

In cutting back the petunias, in removing the dead bits and old overgrown ends, I allow the plants to rejuvenate, to redisperse their energy. In the removal of that which is no longer needed, the petunias have the opportunity to repurpose their life force, becoming more beautiful than before.

In recent years I have come to understand the benefit of pruning my own life, in stripping away that which no longer serves me. In doing so, I clear a path for new growth. I have done this particularly with my habits. I have struggled at times to let go of old ways of being, even when I know they are no longer working. However, when I am finally able to let go of old ideas, old patterns, I find that healthier ones always take their place, always fill the space. In emptiness, I am never lacking.

This year I have learned that pruning is not always personal, internal. That others can provide these snips to my life too. Every relationship I have ever had is like the petal of each petunia; every friend has blessed and brought beauty to my life. Beauty of any kind is never limitless though, and it is important to understand when it is time to let go.

The pruning of plants does not just occur with petunias and other outdoor plants. Inside the greenhouses there is much work to be done too. There is one section of the main greenhouse heavily dedicated to swiss cheese plants. The swiss cheese plant, or monstera adansonii, is a vining climbing beauty with a remarkable leaf pattern. The nickname is apt, with the plant's leaves certainly not unlike the holes found in a block of swiss cheese.

The swiss cheese plants are gorgeous to look at and behave in dramatically different ways dependent on their treatment. Left alone in a pot of soil, the plant will drape down and hang, and the leaves will appear less open. Provided with a moss pole, however, and the stems will send out aerial roots which cling to the pole (not unlike how they would cling to a tree in nature), and the leaves are able to open to their full extent. When given bright, indirect light, all swiss cheese plants grow rapidly.

In the greenhouse, the collection of swiss cheese plants hang as vines as opposed to climbing on poles. There are large pots which hang from ceiling racks and smaller pots which line the bench. Curtains of stems hang and swing from above my head down to puddles of leaves on the floor. Most of the vines of the plants are tremendously long at this point, and it is time for some pruning.

Bonnie walks through the section of swiss cheeses with me, showing me where cuts need to be made. She points out plants with brown or yellow leaves, which need to be removed, and we examine the ones with stems that have collapsed on the floor from length and weight. She explains that I should trim these extended bits back, staggering them so they do not appear to have a bowl cut when the task is complete.

I take my time, carefully cutting away, leaving some stems longer or shorter than others so it appears natural, untouched. Once finished, the plants immediately look refreshed, look happier. They are no longer being dragged down by excess weight and can instead begin branching out at the cuts, producing new growth closer to the roots.

When my friend Darcy comes to visit the garden center, she is drawn to the surreal beauty of these monstera. She decides to purchase one of the planters which hang from above. Weeks later, when I go to visit her in the city, she shows me that she has divided the plant into multiple containers, and gifts me one to take back home.

At home, I am able to prune my swiss cheese even more voraciously than at work. I stagger and pluck bits here and there. Unlike at work, where the excess goes immediately into the compost bin, at home I am able to propagate. I take the bits of stem and leaves that I remove and place them in water on a sunny windowsill. After a few weeks, roots take form. From the pruning, I can both heal the main plant and simultaneously create new ones. In loss, we gain.

I have lost friends before. I have lost friends to death, have lost friends to the natural ebb and flow of a changing life, and I have lost friends when I see that the relationships are no longer beneficial. This year I lose a friend that I was unprepared to lose, a friend I thought would always be a part of my life.

She is a friend I have known for many years, have been

inseparably close with since my second semester of college. We went through a lot together throughout the tenure of our friendship, witnessed the many ups and downs of early adulthood in each other. We held hands, through the joys and through the pains.

After years of my own healing journey, I felt that our friendship was in as solid a state as it had ever been. I felt peace and symbiosis between us. I believed these feelings to be mutual. I learn, unexpectedly, that they are not.

I receive a text message one day that blindsides me. It is a long message, detailing this friend's need to no longer be a part of my life. Whereas most friendships of mine which have ended have done so quietly, naturally, and unsurprisingly, this feels loud, out of the blue, and leaves me in a momentary shock.

I read through her message only once. It is not harsh nor unkind. It is, in fact, full of love. She simply explains that while I myself have healed over the last few years, she has not, and that for her that healing must happen outside of our relationship. Away from me. She thanks me for what I have given her. She says goodbye.

I am simultaneously saddened and relieved. Reading over her words, though initially jarring, I know there is nothing said that is untrue. I have sensed over the last couple of years a misalignment of needs and purpose between us, a chasm that has developed and grown between me and her as we change from our eighteen and nineteen-year-old selves into our twenty-five and twenty-six-year-old selves.

We tried to hold each other's hands over the chasm, have kept grasping despite the natural separation that has been steadily pulling us apart. But the gap was ever-widening, and it became more and more painful to bridge the distance, despite the love we both feel. With her message, her explanation, she finally lets go. I am falling, and I am utterly at peace.

I become a petunia. The petunias do not see the snips coming, nor can they understand the purpose of my sharp fingernails on their throats. They do not understand why they must lose pieces of themselves, why I dispose of their spent blossoms and even remove some healthy new growth.

I become a petunia. I am losing a piece of my heart, one of my closest friends, without warning or understanding. No one explains why the cuts must be made. Yet even if I do not have immediate perspective, cannot yet see the situation from above, I see it in the flowers. I see it in myself: this is for my own good. This is for the growth of it all.

Pruning opens up possibility. When we cut back a plant, when we remove unseemly, unhealthy sections, we do not know exactly what will happen. We cannot control the growth, only encourage it. The same is true in my life. When I lose parts of myself—friends whom I cherish, habits that have allowed me to survive but not thrive, old ways of thinking which I assumed were integral to my being—it feels exactly like that: a loss.

Where the petunias recover from this loss in days, flourishing and blossoming more fully than before over the course of a single weekend, my own replenishment requires more patience. It can take weeks, months, years for new growth to become visible. It can take ages to understand why the pruning had to happen. And yet each time, no matter how long it takes, the value is always apparent.

When parts of my life are removed, by my hand or the hand of another or by the mysterious flow of Mother Nature herself, it creates a vacuum. And if there is one thing that plants have taught me it is that no empty patch of soil can stay that way for long.

New people flow in to fill the spaces, relationships that are more fruitful, more aligned with my current state. New and healthier habits enter to replace older, less effective ones. And, most importantly, I have more space, more energy, more time. There is space to be with myself, to learn from my own body and mind. I let myself fill the void, and I let myself fall in love with these new pieces of my life.

I become a petunia. I am full, lush, and constantly ready to release new blooms. In order to do so, in order to always be putting out new growth, I need a little trim every now and then. When I do not give myself this pruning, Mother Nature always finds her way.

Throughout the summer season, I return many times over to my very first task: pruning the mint. Mint grows prolifically—it can be invasive in the garden as a result. This is because it roots itself absolutely everywhere. You can witness this yourself with ease. Simply take a cutting of mint stem several inches long, lay it on top of some soil in a pot, and place the whole thing in the sunshine. Within days it will begin to root.

Every time I go to trim the mint, it is entangled within itself. One pot is attached to the next is attached to the next and so on, each plant rooting anywhere it can find bare soil, creating an intricate web of stems and aromatic leaves. The plants are lanky, overgrown, searching.

I work, as I usually do, one by one, bit by bit. I trim each plant, stem by stem, removing generous lengths. I mourn the pieces which drop into my compost bin, thank them for the nutrient-rich humus they will soon become. I go through every mint plant, dozens upon dozens, until they have all been tended to. Then, I wait.

Over the course of each week following a hefty mint pruning, I check in on the plants religiously. I take special care to pass through the herb-filled bench mart several times a day, keen to witness their progress.

I am always disappointed at first, and even slightly alarmed by what I see. When the mint grows lanky, the base of the plants become bare. Now, snipped back to the bareness, the lack of leaves is glaringly apparent. This is how I feel after I lose pieces of my life, how I feel after losing my best friend. Barren. Unsightly. Utterly vulnerable. The mints are crying out. *Look at us! What have you done? What is the purpose of this?* I cannot explain it to them yet, but I feel their pain.

After a week, however, things look drastically different. I return to the herbs and am repeatedly amazed by the transformation. Where bare stems stood just days ago, an abundant crowding of redolent green has appeared. Not only are the old cut back stems covered in lush leaves, but small new stems are appearing all over the base. The mint was spending so much energy holding onto old parts that there was no energy left for new growth. By forcing the mint to let go of old growth patterns, I pave the way for it to have a fuller, healthier future.

I am indescribably thankful to this former friend of mine. I am thankful for all the beauty she brought into my life over the years. I am thankful she held my hand for that part of my journey. And I am thankful that when the time was right, she saw and did what I could not. She decided: this is no longer healthy, no longer serving us. It is time to let go.

When I receive the message from her, I know she is uncertain of how I will react. I write back to her, briefly, and tell her I think what she has said is beautiful. I mean it. She wants to heal, to change, to grow, and she realized she cannot do that alongside me. I love her, want the best for her, and so I tell her how genuinely excited I am for this new part of her journey. I am thrilled for her, to shed that which no longer aids her on her path, to grow and change and blossom, even if I will not be there to witness it. Knowing that it is happening at all is enough.

I want this friend to do anything that will be healing for her, because healing, as I have come to learn, is one of the most beautiful gifts we can give ourselves. I want her to heal, and so I am in complete support of her choice to end our friendship. What I see now is that this act of pruning on her part is healing me as well.

Her absence opens a void, a vacuum—a welcome one. It opens a space within me. Space to reflect, space to love, space to write these very words. It allows me to return to my roots, to send out new growth from my base, from my center, from a place of my deepest truth, rather than continue down the same paths simply because they are well worn, well known.

Just as the mint must be maintained consistently, so must I pinch back for a lifetime the pieces of my being that no longer serve me. I welcome the task. Just as the mint is wild, will grow back in whichever manner it pleases, I know that my growth is also unlimited, undefined, uncontainable. I do not know where my path will lead. I do not want to pretend to have all the answers, or any answers at all. Instead, I will simply continue to tend to the garden of my life, carefully clearing space for new growth, new people and places, new ideas.

I do not know what to expect once I do. I do not know what the future holds, what seeds exist in my body that are waiting to burst forth once they have the space and energy to do so. I do not know. All I know for certain is this: beauty blossoms in the voids.

Trees

SPRING IS a strange time in the natural world. It is a time of emergence, of beginnings, and there is a certain hope to it—but there is also a darkness present, something haunting. I don't want this to be true—that there could be something to fear in spring—but the air feels heavy with caution.

Spring, like autumn, is a bridge between death and life. Autumn as such a bridge feels natural. We watch as the leaves on trees die and fall, as the early frosts hit the petals of perennials and they retreat to the soil, with only the root systems remaining alive and dormant underground. In autumn, we see life play out in a straightforward and sensical way: whole and breathing and then, hit with an outside force, dying and dead. We walk the bridge of autumn straight into winter, bundle ourselves up in blankets and fire, and cocoon within the warmth of family and friends and lovers. Autumn carries us there, to dormancy, to rest, to a momentary death. Autumn is the same as dying, and this I understand.

Spring, another bridge, confounds and unsettles me. Spring is the bridge away from death and toward life, and I struggle to find peace in that, struggle to understand. I watch as tulips and daffodils poke their heads out of barely warmed grounds. I see the first leaves of the hydrangeas form out of woody and seemingly static bases. I watch as the trees overhead begin to fill out, as life returns to the air around me. This is hopeful, this is beautiful, and yet, there is a deep loneliness to this time of year.

Whereas in autumn we are joining as one, transforming the individual into the collective time and time again—pumpkin patch gatherings, leaves huddled in piles, coming together as a group by the hearth—spring portends isolation.

The first of the brave animals poking their heads out. The first of the cooped-up humans venturing out, too. The plants, thawed, jutting their green tips through the soil. I watch the ones that come up too early and I mourn—they do not know that the potential for frost has yet to retreat, that there is still death present, creeping up behind them. They do not know that they should be afraid as they race toward the vibrancy of summer. Spring is a lonely time.

The bridge that is spring is heavy with rain and possibility and fear. There is a violence to birth, something terrifying in the beauty of new life, and this season holds that tension with precision. There is a comfort and calm in the stillness of winter, one that spring breaks open with force every year. It is the most natural thing, and yet it feels untenable, unfathomable. I am afraid of spring. I am afraid of hope.

It is here in this time of uncertainty and bravery and fear that I find myself walking through the expanses of the New York Botanical Garden. My parents and I drive up to the Bronx one Sunday morning in April, wanting to visit the garden while the daffodils and other early blooms are in full swing. From Connecticut it is a quick drive, and we arrive at the main entrance before the gardens have opened.

The daffodils do not disappoint. Fields of creamy yellow flowers cover hills of green. We bathe in the vibrant array of the narcissus, each variety slightly different in style and hue. Daffodils, some of the first blooms of spring, offer their bright and sunny faces to me. *Be not afraid, Eleanor*, I hear them say. *You are prepared for what's to come.*

Though it is still early in the season, and many plants lay dormant beneath the surface of the soil, there is still plenty of beauty to be seen. The lilac bushes are a particular treat to wander around. The stunning purple and pink shades of these plants are outperformed only by the gorgeous aroma they emit. The magnolia trees are another showstopper. Impossible to miss, huge walls of white and pink blossoms line a wide walking path. Many of the blooms are spent, and a delightful dance of delicate petals pattern the ground. Early spring's attempt at snow: flowers falling and collecting like so many flakes in a storm.

My parents and I wander through the expanse of the massive property for hours, marveling at each sign of life. My father is impressed by the lettuces, practical cold-weather plants that here have been arranged in gorgeous patterns—rabbit food made into art. I am lucky to be the child of two people who value nature as much as I do. I am vastly different from both of my parents, and they from each other, and yet, we all always have this to return to: our shared wonder at the green and growing gifts the Earth provides.

We three, mother, father, and daughter, are somber as we explore. Our visit to NYBG comes just days after our precious family dog has passed away. We are all mourning, silently so, and we all allow ourselves to be caressed and carried by the abundant life around us. In death, it is important to recall that life continues on.

The gardens are full of flowering plants of every imaginable kind, some in bloom, some still waiting their turn. I love flowers, shrubs, native plants, all the beauty that the gardens provide. Where I feel most at home, however, is amongst the trees. The botanical garden contains a plethora of woodsy areas full of these towering friends. When we depart from the flowering fields and enter the forest, I breathe in, breathe out. I am home.

We meander slowly through the woods, pausing to watch a bird here or there flit among the trees, listening to the flow of waterways at the path's edge. The quiet of the trees holds me, holds my grief and my love, and I am grateful. I am honored.

We pause, too, to read the various plaques that line the walking paths, gleaning information about the history of the gardens, about the trees, about the land we stand on. We soak it all in. Mostly I look over the posted information quickly, gulping up the knowledge each sign provides. At one plaque, however, I linger. I read it over and over again. It feels like it was written by the forest itself, just for me.

I do not take a picture of the sign to revisit later. I do not need to. The meaning of the text becomes embedded in my soul. This is what it teaches me: *Dead trees are an essential piece of the forest.* When a tree falls, it fills many important roles. The dead, fallen tree provides shelter for animals. As the tree decomposes, it provides essential nutrients that rejuvenate all the plants of the forest. And finally, the falling of a dead tree clears an opening in the canopy. Younger, smaller trees that were not able to receive as much light before are now able to access the energy the sun provides, with a wide space in the canopy newly opened. These young trees, now that they have more access to light, are able to grow, to reach previously impossible heights.

I am stunned by what I read, what I learn. This idea holds me. The death of trees is essential to forest health, particularly for the younger trees. This notion immediately becomes a metaphor for my grandmother's passing. It feels like more than a metaphor, though. It feels like truth.

When I learn this about the trees, the necessity of death for new life, I am able to see how essential Dede's death was for the younger trees that surround her: her daughter (my mother) and me. While her death is devastating, in the moment and to this day, I can see how necessary it is.

My mother and I have always had a complicated relationship. With Dede's death, we are washed over in clarity, and the pettiness between us starts to evaporate. Dede's death, the lessons it gives, becomes nourishment for the relationship between us. It is what allows us to heal the space, mend the wounds. Just as the tree falling allows light to peek in and down toward the younger trees, Dede's death lets light in, lets us see the brightness and beauty in each other. Gives us the energy to grow.

When Dede dies, just as the pieces of a tree break down to feed the forest around it, the pieces of Dede's spirit, and her body itself, nurture those around her. Her compassion—her innate capacity to treat everyone with loving kindness—floats through the air and attaches to all those who love her. Her sense of humor, inappropriate at times, pours over us each in bouts of laughter. Her beauty will henceforth feed and live on in every blade of grass, every hummingbird, every oak tree. There are no goodbyes in the forest. There is only a single family, one with an ever-changing portrait.

Dede's death nurtures, nurtures the lives of the people she loves, the people who love her. I mourn Dede, just as I mourn a tree, and at the same time, I understand it is an essential part of life. That she is not gone, but simply transformed. Her body feeds the flowers, and her soul feeds us all. The trees teach me, teach me that death is not an end. It is the beginning. It is the source of all life. Death is, in its own way, a home.

Trees are always teaching me, have stood as my silent leaders for years. They teach me how to ground myself, how to reach into the Earth for peace. They teach me presence, a topic I become obsessed with, confounded by. There are two books I read, both of which guide me in my quest for the present moment (sweet irony noted). *Be Here Now* by Ram Dass and *The Power of Now* by Eckhart Tolle. There are certain books I read that feel like I wrote them, and they feel this way because I have. There are some writers, thinkers, who are able to tap into truths that I believe exist in all our cores—in the core of the universe. Truths that we each wrote, understood, long before we were born.

As I read these books, I feel this: I wrote this. I wrote these words, and they are truth, and here we are. The message at the core of both books is simple, and it is the same. Enlightenment is happening, and all one must do to access it is be here, be now. Be present. Be.

I read the words in these books and it's like getting high without drugs, without anything at all, just a natural high state within myself. It is truth. I see it in small practices. I see how when I allow myself to be present, to fully hold myself in the current moment, all pain, all worries, all shame fades away. There is only here. Only now. Only me and the current sensations in my body. I am alive. There is only joy in that, in every moment.

One of my favorite questions to ask people becomes this: when you are avoiding the present, are you doing so by living in the past or in the future? I enjoy watching the people I love ponder this idea, and I can always guess at their answer.

For as long as I can recall, I have lived my life looking backward, eyes facing the rearview mirror. I have always been submerged in the past, shrouded in memory and pain. Depression, shame—these ailments stem from glancing over my shoulder, from my refusal to dig into the here, into the now.

While those looking backward tend to be depressives, like me, I find that those who avoid the present by looking toward the future tend to be anxious types. I can picture one friend of mine, a lovely man who holds more anxiety in his body than almost anyone I know. His mind is consistently racing forward, chasing the next, worrying. Rather than existing in the now, those of us plagued by the future are racing ahead, missing the current moment for the unpromised possibility of another.

Of course, most of us jump back and forth, daydreaming or worrying about the future one minute, consumed by nostalgia or shame of the past in the next. Whether forward or backward-looking, negative or positive in design, these are all the same tools, the same practice. Avoidance. Avoidance of the here and now, avoidance of the body, of the physical and emotional sensations coursing through us in every instant. So many of us, so much of the time, are avoiding the present. Avoiding life.

I want to learn how to live in the present. I can sense that many of my troubles in life have stemmed from avoidance, from a refusal to be with my current state. I want to learn how to sit with myself, how to face the now, how to stop running from pain.

I meditate. I practice yoga, intuitive stretching. I learn breathing exercises. I read *The Power of Now, Be Here Now*, both of which reinforce for me the importance of honoring nature, learning from nature. These books teach me invaluable lessons, but I am still missing a link. All my practices open a window for me, develop an opening inside my sightline. I get closer to what feels like my own personal truth, and then am pulled further from it the second it is within grasp. I am lacking. My ideas are floating, my sense of spirituality spinning through the air. I lack grounding.

I work with a healer. She is a shaman, one I found many years ago through my therapist and have spent several sessions with since. I work with her when I feel like I need a push in my healing, a bit of guidance. I reach out to her this summer after doing my readings and my meditations and still finding there is a piece of the puzzle missing.

I reach out to her and tell her: *I want to learn to be more present.* She laughs at me, lovingly and not unexpectedly. I have big dreams.

She guides me. She tells me I am always here, always present, even if it does not feel like it. I take this in, hold it to my chest.

She tells me the next time I am losing my sense of presence to ask: *Who is here?*

I begin to practice this regularly. I check in with nature, with the world around me, and see who else is present with me at any given moment. I ask, silently or aloud, who's here (with me)? I ask, and I am always answered.

A few days later, the shaman checks in with me via email, asks me how I am doing. I respond: *I have been doing well since we spoke. "Who's here?" has become my new mantra (I've actually gotten in the habit of asking "chi è qui?" because I love the way the words flow in Italian). Each time I ask, I inevitably see a tree. I have been and continue to be so mesmerized by trees—these beings that have had their roots in the ground since before I was born and many of whom will remain long after I'm gone. I ask who's here, chi è qui, and I see the trees that surround me always, and I feel my feet sink deeper into the ground. My feet get heavier, more solid, and it's as though I myself am rooting. Rooting into the present moment, rooting into the earth, rooting into the rhythm and flow of the nature that surrounds me, that I am intrinsically a part of.*

I am learning to be more playful as I also learn to be more present. I have been laughing at myself more, remembering that even when I feel myself floating away—there I am! You're trying so hard to be present, and yet you don't have to try at all. Here you are. Here you are! Standing and solid and here, and just exactly right, in this moment. Every moment.

Every time I lose myself, every time that I need a reminder, all I must do is ask: who's here? *Chi è qui?* There is always a tree around to let me know: *You are never alone. You are always held, here and now.*

A few years ago, while I was at an inpatient PTSD treatment program in Arizona, I was introduced to therapeutic ideas that changed my life. The program I attended was a remarkable one, and I was exposed to a multitude of modalities. I was also educated on trauma, on the psychology and physiology of it, and on why trauma lingers in the body.

I learned that when we experience something traumatic, our bodies can store the energy from the trauma in unhealthy ways. This is how I arrived at treatment. I experienced something traumatic, and my body did not know what to do with the energy of it all. I wound up with insomnia, panic attacks, anxiety, suicidal ideation. My body believed itself to be constantly in danger, and I was always on edge as a result.

One of my therapists was incredible, and worked heavily in the realm of images. I made great strides in her office, allowing my body and the images that arose within me to direct my healing process. I spent this time drawing pictures, expressing the visions and colors that lived in different parts of my body, and coming to understand my body as healing, whole, alive, and, most importantly, as myself—rather than as the unforgiving enemy I had come to understand it as.

One day, my therapist tasked me with crafting different images to represent the different parts of me. She told me on this day, as she often did, not to think about it too deeply, to just put down on paper the first images that came to mind. I did as she said, closing my eyes, letting the images roll, pressing pen to paper.

The first thing I saw was in the pit of my stomach, all curled up. I pictured this part of myself as an ant. This piece of me was so small, so perplexed by the world around her. This little ant inside of me was strong for her size, powerful in her own right, but no match for the forces of the world. I told my therapist: *This is the traumatized part of me. She just feels so small, so confused.*

The next image was simple, just a sad, hurt face. This was the childlike part of me, I realized. Her face looked bleak, devoid of hope, and utterly, palpably, alone.

I found catharsis in discovering these parts of myself, in crafting images for the traumatized piece of me, the child in me, as well as other images for my depressed part, my jealous part, my self-soothing part. All the different pieces of me, gifted with names and images and colors and scenes, all to help make myself whole, bring me home.

My therapist pressed me to create one more image, one imagining. She asked me, now that I had laid out all the structures within me, to envision a future version of myself. A more adult, more centered, more authentic part of me. An image to strive for. I began to draw.

I am not much of a visual artist, and so my attempt was simple. Two long smooth lines, slightly curved. A massive canopy of leaves. I, before ever learning or knowing about plants or presence or anything to do with the green things of this Earth, had drawn my adult self as a tree.

My therapist asked me to explain this. Little explanation was necessary, for her or me; it is innate. When I envisioned the person I wanted to become at the time (the person I think I now may just be), I saw a tree. I saw my feet; I saw roots planted firmly in the ground. I felt the whole of my body connected to the whole of the Earth. I felt my legs and core and arms spread out as the limbs of a tree, my breadth creating simultaneous shade and glow.

My therapist took this visual and created it into an exercise, one that I still practice to this day. She had me stand up, spread my feet so they were placed comfortably under my hips. Then, she asked me to squat down, to bend my knees at a sharp angle so I lost about half a foot of height. She then took my hands, placed them atop my head, and asked me to close my eyes. She told me to use my hands to push down against the top of my head, to create pressure. I did this. Then, she asked me to imagine myself as the tree.

I did this, too. Eyes closed, hands pressing down, I was the tree. I felt my feet rooting into the ground beneath me, stretching out, gaining balance and support. I felt my core, my trunk, lengthen and strengthen. And finally, when I was ready, I began to push up and out against the weight of my hands against my head. I pushed, pushed, until I could feel the force of my body winning, until I was reaching and moving toward the heavens, the sun, the light. I practiced this over and over again, embodying the tree, remembering my roots. I know now in plain English what I knew then, at my most traumatized, only at my unconscious core: to be a tree is to be present. To be present is to heal.

I am often left staring at trees in wonder, so I am blessed to live in a home surrounded by them. Our family home is situated across the street from a beautiful river and woods, a gorgeous patch of land protected by the town and left relatively undisturbed. These woods extend not only across the street from my house but down the road as well, and the result is a plethora of woodlands all around me, and a mass of trees in some form always within eyesight.

Staring out at the tree branches one day from my bedroom window, I think about the power that these creatures have. They are massive, omnipresent. I imagine what it must be like to be a tree, to experience the world from so high up and simultaneously from its core, its roots deep within the Earth. To feel and know the movements of the world on every level, every plane. What peace there must be in that sort of presence. I imagine there to be great loneliness in standing as a tree, and great love.

I learn this year that trees communicate with each other. While I feel I should be stunned by this fact, the opposite is true. I am calmed by this idea, and immediately am overcome by a sense of understanding and relief. Of course they do. Of course they do.

I come to learn that there are two primary channels of communication that trees use: air and land. Through the air, trees release pheromones in order to get their message across. Through land, trees utilize an underground fungal network that connects to the root systems. These routes of quiet conversation allow the trees to warn each other of danger, communicate needs, and even pass nutrients to one another in order to support the weaker members of the community.

I am fascinated by this, by the linguistics of branches and roots. Around the same time that I am learning about tree communication, I revisit a favorite novella of mine, *Story of Your Life* by Ted Chiang. It is a heartbreaking and simultaneously calming work that ponders what aliens might have to teach in the realm of language, what their differences might pull forth from us.

Ted Chiang is a genius. In each of his works, he creates what the best of science fiction allows for: speculative tales about the expansiveness of existence, cautionary and hopeful in nature, and always enthralling, always pushing me to see the world through a different lens. Every word he writes helps explode new ways of thinking in my mind, creating pathways from nothing like dynamite in a mine.

In *Story of Your Life*, Chiang's narrative is one in which an alien language has the capacity to alter the way users of the language perceive time. Because our human narrator successfully learns to communicate using the alien tongue, her mind is utterly transformed.

I begin to see the trees as their own kind of aliens. These creatures who are so vastly different from us, with bodies made of bark and cork and wood, yet who are just as alive as us, just as present. Just as real. I want to play with the possibility that they know more, that their communication has something to teach us. I wonder: what would it look like if trees, just like the aliens in Chiang's story, were able to help us understand their form of language? What would it look like if I learned to speak through my roots, my body, my branches?

What would it look like if you could feel my pain through my feet? If you innately felt this pain through pulses in your toes? If you could send me nutrients, supplies, and energy in order to help me heal? What if I could do the same for you? I wonder, what could trees teach us about our place in the world, about forming community, about being a part of something grander than ourselves, if only we could hear them?

I walk through the woods near my house one day. I want to write, want to write exactly what I am writing right now, but I feel blocked. I feel I am not able to communicate. I am not certain what I *want* to communicate. So, I walk to the woods. I put everything down and return to the cradle that has held me so many times before. I ask it to hold me once more. I ask it to teach me. This time, I am listening.

I am gifted an answer, so simple, so perfect: silence. Trees communicate, and trees form community, and trees create the basis and homes for so much of the life on Earth. Trees create and give and communicate, and they do all of it in total silence.

I stand in the center of the woods and look around me. I look up. I see the light filter through the branches, see the enormity of the trunks waving in the wind, see the insects and birds and squirrels who have made their habitats in the bark, have found safety here. I look, and I see so much. I listen, and I hear nothing.

The trees live in silence, and yet they communicate. I try to grasp this, the intensity of this, the possibilities this opens up in my own life. I speak so much, am talking talking talking, but often I am saying very little. Speaking for the sake of it. What could it look like to save communication, to savor it? To live in silence and to still spread the ideas that require urgency?

To share and spread knowledge, wisdom, life, without sparing a single breath?

In *Be Here Now*, Ram Dass speaks about silence, about his spiritual teacher who taught him using only chalk and a small blackboard. He speaks about the value of this, what is distilled from silence. In silence, we can filter out that which is meaningless, superfluous. In silence, we can pull forth the truth of life.

The trees reinforce this. Reteach this. They have created a community, a form of civilization, cityscapes, and worlds unto themselves. Forests. They have done all this, worked in tandem, without uttering a word.

The trees show me that all the communication that is necessary can be done quietly, purposefully. The trees show me to communicate with love and intention. The trees show me that their communication is exactly how they make me feel present. That their silence, their resilience, their presence, are all one in the same.

There is presence in silence, in physical silence and the silence of one's mind. When we free ourselves from fretting about the future, free ourselves from the plague of the past, free ourselves from thought and speech as a whole, there is only now, only here. When I let my mind quiet, let my mouth quiet, there is only this body that I find myself one with, and only this gorgeous world, perfect exactly as it is, here, now. I find myself one with this, too.

I often feel guilty, or at least guilty in vocalizing, that I do believe the Earth is perfect exactly as it is, right in this moment. I feel guilty because when life is painful, it is hard to see that pain, and the whole of nature it exists within, as beautiful. Perfect. I understand this. And yet I do believe it to be true. That the Earth is perfect in every moment.

I believe that everything is exactly as it should be. I believe this only because I do not understand nature, but I love her. I love this beautiful world that I am a part of, and so while I am often perplexed by her, frustrated or saddened, I trust that I am held—held by the universe. When I quiet my mind, when I stop worrying about what the future may bring, stop regretting the past, I am able to slip into the quiet present timeline of the trees, of the universe as a whole: here, now, standing tall, witnessing the movements of the Earth from the clouds to the core.

I work on developing a practice of silence. I am trying to be more silent, mentally and externally, in order to be here. When I say it is a practice, it is one that I will work on my entire life. I do not think I will ever be entirely quiet. Nor do I wish to be. What I wish to do is try. Try to spend more moments each day clearing my mind of chaos. Try to relax into the present. Try to ask: *Who's here?* I will try to remember that there is presence in silence. I will try to look up toward the trees and see the value in a quiet communication.

I begin to wonder if trees would write if they could. I wonder if this is what they're doing in a sense. Their silent form of communication versus mine. They carve the story of the world into the Earth. I carve the story of my life into the page. Does the world stand still as I write? Does each letter represent a single moment, a root reaching into soil?

I used to have a much harder time writing. I loved it, yet I would have to force myself to do it, and would judge it and myself if I did not believe my words were any "good." I have learned through the trees that there is no such thing as good or bad communication, no such thing as a good or bad existence at all. There is just being. There is just doing. All of it is right, simply because it is.

Now writing flows from me, the way a tree grows. Look at any tree anywhere and you will find that it is not symmetrical nor pristine. It has asymmetrical branches, markings along its trunk, haphazard leanings, and curves. And still, despite its humanized imperfection, it grows exactly as it should. It communicates exactly as it needs to. It knows its place in the world, and the world holds its place.

I let my words flow the way I watch the trees grow. I do not know when this shifted; I only know that it did. That I now no longer need my words to be perfect, or good, or necessary in order for them to exist at all. They exist because I am part of the world, like the trees, and I too can communicate in silence if I so please.

I wish I had understood that earlier in life, that I can create simply because I want to. Simply because some part of me needs my creation to exist. I have spent so much of my life communicating superfluously in the ways I thought I was supposed to. Now I am learning to be like the trees, to communicate silently, to spread only that which is pertinent, to say only that which I wish and not an utterance more. I am learning. I am learning, too, to not judge what naturally flows forth from me. There is no more room to apologize for feeling. Let it all be fodder for creation.

I can build a world around me. I can create without permission. Like every tree in the forest, all art is beautiful because it captures the now. Every tree is perfect because it exists here and now. Every work of art is right because it captures the mind in a single moment. It allows for the creator to release it, that moment. To secure it in the past, the future, to send the regrets or worries to one of those places and to thus be able to live wholly, solidly: here and now.

That is my hope with all these words here. That I may write down my learnings, my losses, and leave them here, in this space, this time. I pray to leave all my regret in the past and all my hope in the future. I pray that this creation creates room for more creation, and so on and so forth until the day I die, and my body becomes creative material from which new trees can grow.

The magnitude of trees is hard for me to grasp, though I try anyway. My dad one day points out the huge tree in our front yard. He points it out while we are driving home. Coming up the street, it does look absolutely massive.

He points it out because it is mid-October, and the leaves are the most gorgeous and vibrant orange that either of us has ever seen. My dad says: *The tree never looks this good. The leaves are always so brown.* This time, perfectly orange, steadily falling.

As we pull into the driveway, I can see that more than half

the yard has already been raked up. My dad is always so proud of his lawn, green and bright in the summer, well-maintained the rest of the year. His yard is usually a solo masterpiece. This year, I encroach, planting as much as I can in the carefully sculpted beds of mulch and soil and trees.

I look up at this tree, this massive beauty that has stood in our front yard for as long as I have been alive. I look at its decadent orange display and avoid saying what is obvious to my eyes. The tree is not brown this year because it is putting on a show. The tree is orange this year because it knows I am home. I do not have to say this part aloud. Some things are just known—a wink between Mother Nature and I.

I go for walks in the woods by my house whenever I need to clear my mind, to recenter, reground. One of the entrances to the woods has a small wooden board for postings, one of which describes a Japanese term: *Shinrin-yoku*. The paper reads: "shinrin-yoku / *Japanese noun* 森林浴 / n. translated in English as 'forest bathing.'" Moving softly through trees as a means of healing the body, the mind, the soul.

I play with this concept in my head throughout my walks. I am comforted to know that humans the world over see the beauty of forests, their necessity, their healing powers. I am comforted to know that humans have created whole words for just that, that healing.

Every step I take through a forest, I find them swallowing up my pain. They take that which is broken in me and say here, child, unburden. Feel your body, feel your bones. I cry, I laugh, I return home.

There is so much that is unnatural nowadays about human existence. So much that removes us from the flow of the world. Walking through a forest, amongst the trees, is like being called back. Trees remind me that I always have a home in the natural world.

One day I find myself paralyzingly overwhelmed by the realities of climate change, by the harm humans, as a species, have done to our planet. I also, congruently, find myself overwhelmed by the casual unwillingness of people to see themselves as a part of nature, the tendency toward individualism at the expense of a collective ecological health.

I witness this firsthand at my job. I am lucky that not only do I work at a garden center, but I also happen to work at one that is situated adjacent to a massive pond, a pond that is a part of the same ecosystem of woods and river which flows by my house. I am so lucky, and it also makes perfect sense. That the universe would tie my life together in these ways, with these perfect winking bows of woodland and water, wrapped up just for me.

At work, I learn that some of the other people whose properties also back up onto the open space have been clear-cutting trees. The trees are town property and belong to us all—and particularly to the woodland critters that rely on these plants for their food and shelter. People want a beautiful view of the pond, however, and so they cut away the trees that block this view. No consideration for the toll it takes, the harm it will do.

It is my boss who explains this to me, with anger in her voice. The way people carelessly cut down the nature in their backyards. I find myself incensed, an unusual feeling for me. I want to cry. We have so little open space left, here in my town and in the world as a whole. And here people go, chopping it down. When it's all gone, where will we go?

I decide I need to do something to remedy this injustice, but I do not know what. My boss has tried to reach out to the town for years, with little success. I do not know who to ask for help, where to turn for guidance. So, I go to the place the trees have shown me. I enter the realm of silence. I spend time in the silence, ask her what to do, and she tells me. Sow seeds.

I am so overwhelmed by the careless disregard for trees, nature. I am overwhelmed by my fears of our heating planet, by the massive hand humans have had in our own destruction. I am overwhelmed, and I am terrified, and I feel so very small. So, I start smaller than I feel, and I procure acorns.

I decide I want white oak acorns because white oaks are remarkably good at absorbing and utilizing carbon from the air and storing it in the ground. They can live for centuries and can help us all to breathe better, and so I decide to purchase fifty acorns. I decide to plant as a declaration of hope, as a way to say: I believe a better future is possible. I also decide to plant as a way to quell anxiety, to not worry if a better future is possible, or even if a future is possible at all. I plant to be present, to place an acorn in the ground, here and now, without any expectation beyond it being there, today.

I purchase the acorns in early fall, and they sit in my room until mid-January. After I buy them, I am confronted by a sense of doubt. It all feels pointless. Silly. It feels like throwing sprinkles of water onto a raging gas fire. Hopeful is a scary thing to be.

While these acorns sit in my room, patiently awaiting a decision or action on my part, I stumble upon another book. I am in the city for my twenty-sixth birthday, exploring a bookshop with a friend after brunch, when I discover it: *Sowing Seeds in the Desert* by Masanobu Fukuoka. I find this book in one of those serendipitous ways, one of those ways that tell you the universe is laughing, and you are in on the joke.

I am standing here, on my birthday, telling my friend about desertification. I am telling her about how it feels so pressing to me, how humans have desecrated the soil to the point of erosion, how soil is becoming sand, everywhere and rapidly. I tell her that it feels like I am being pulled toward this topic, that it keeps popping up in different texts and documentaries that I engage with. The idea is everywhere: save our soil, save us all.

It is as I am talking, wildly, about desertification, that I find *Sowing Seeds in the Desert*. I am immediately moved by the soft colors of the cover, and even before reading the back (which, of course, includes a recommendation from Toby Hemenway, the author of another transcendent book, *Gaia's Garden*), I know that this book must come home with me.

Every page of Fukuoka's book resonates. It feels once again

like reading *Be Here Now* or *The Power of Now*. Ah, I say. I wrote this. Another part of my heart, another piece of this universe that I am a part of, sat down with these thoughts and wrote these words just for me, so I can have them now and create beauty with them here. Reading *Sowing Seeds in the Desert* feels like remembering. It feels like my body returning to itself. I am being called home.

The biggest takeaway I get from this book is that nature can heal herself, is *trying* to heal herself. All we must do is stop creating damage and take a step back. In the places where the damage we have done is tremendous, we cannot abandon nature. Rather, we must step in and step up, provide her with the tools to heal, and then remove ourselves from the decision-making process, relinquish control. This is of the utmost urgency.

Fukuoka explains that humans believe our intelligence entitles us to control the Earth, to control nature. He laments that in doing so, we stop understanding our place in nature, do not consider how far-reaching and catastrophic our actions are.

The book allows for the possibility of a different kind of Earth. It reminds us that the Earth was at one time an Eden, a paradise, and that if we so choose, if we can let ourselves see the truth of nature, we might just be able to restore it. We must trust that nature knows more than us, has a grander plan than we can conceive of—a bigger and more bountiful story to tell than the one we have tried to create. Instead of attempting to control nature, we must step back and let her operate in peace, in harmony. If we allow nature to restore herself, we can be restored simultaneously. In healing nature, we can heal our bodies, our spirits, too.

Inspired by the words of Fukuoka, inspired by all the people like him who can see the beauty of the Earth and seek to honor that, I get to work. I place my acorns in a canvas tote bag, one with an image of two bright red cherries on the side. I layer myself in tights, jeans, and a sweater and bundle up in a puffy green jacket and scarf for good measure. To the forest we go.

I decide not to plant the acorns, or at least not in the

way I originally intend. When I first purchased the acorns, I pictured myself with a trowel, carefully digging perfect holes for each one, backfilling them, photographing each location, and coming back to check on them all next year.

I decide instead to relinquish control. I want to add these acorns into the woods, want to aid in replenishing the trees that have been clear cut and destroyed, yet I realize: who am I to say where these acorns belong, who and how they will best serve? Who am I to say that these acorns are even supposed to become trees at all? Instead of planting them, carefully and precisely (without truthfully having a framework for where or why), I scatter them. I grab a handful of acorns, and I scatter them. I decide: let nature guide the way. I continue scattering acorns as I walk until my bag is empty. I sit by the pond for a while. I return home.

Maybe the acorns will all grow up to be spectacular trees, each providing shade and comfort and carbon sequestration for centuries to come. Most likely, however, this will not come to pass. I must accept that most of these acorns will probably become food for animals, some may fall over and into the river's edge, and others may simply decompose, becoming food for fungus which will recycle their nutrients. In coming to accept this, that not all my acorns can become trees, I am also able to learn and accept another important fact: that not all acorns are *supposed* to become trees.

Acorns are oak seeds, of course, but they are also food. They are both. And there is such beauty in saying: I am not going to decide which is more valuable. I am not going to decide anything at all. I am going to thrust nature back into nature, because it's all one in the same, and then I am going to close my eyes and turn away and trust that without my hand, everything will run its course exactly as it's meant to.

I am trying to learn to give in this way, love in this way— generously, unabashedly, without prejudice. I am always learning that I have much to learn, in terms of loving. I am a lifelong student, never a master. I am learning that some days, loving a single plant or a single patch of woods can be lesson enough. To heal one is to heal all. I am learning. I am loving. I am healing.

I am lucky that so much healing has entered my life, has been brought to me by so many beautiful people, places, and philosophies. I am particularly grateful that I was introduced to these tools at such a young age, and now have a full life ahead of me to apply and amend these practices. A whole life centered on growing. A fuller life, I cannot hope for.

At my treatment program in Arizona and beyond, I came to understand that so much of what traumatizes us is physical. So much of our daily pains result from avoidance and negligence of our physical forms and our disconnection from nature. Returning to the body, healing the myriad parts of the body, learning what pains they hold—this is the beginning. This is how we heal, nature and ourselves.

Trauma is a hyper-lack of presence. It is living, viscerally, in the past and in fear of the future. It is a demand on the body to split itself open between these two immensely painful worlds.

To heal the body, to heal trauma, we must help ourselves return to the present, return to the now. This can be terrifying, to engage with one's physical sensations when the body feels so raw, so petrified, but there is great grace and beauty in returning to the physical. Tremendous healing to be found here.

I learn that every piece of me is valuable. That to be ashamed of a piece of myself is like mocking the base of a seventy-foot-tall tree. How can I chastise its base, its roots, while marveling at its overarching height, its current glory? Did the gangly lower trunk and bespeckled branches not allow for this beauty? Did the awe of today not require the grit and struggle of years prior?

One of my therapists, a lovely woman who I know I would not be here without, one day drew a circle on a piece of paper. She wanted to show me, me. Show me who I was. I was lacking in perspective, and she wanted to gift me a bird's eye view, and healthy momentum. She drew a circle, and, in the center, she wrote my first name: Eleanor. Around it, in a second circle, she wrote out the traits of my youth: inquisitive, kind, thoughtful, caring, generous, loving, silly, playful, good. Then, she drew another circle, and here she wrote out the traits of my present self, as well as some of the hardships I was enduring.

She drew an arrow, from the outer edge of the paper all the way to the center, to Eleanor, tracing along all the positive traits and remarking on all the resilience I've shown, all I'd endured along the way. She traced to the center, and I saw: I can always access this. This middle part. The center of me. My true self. She is always here, always waiting.

There is no shame, because at my core, I am still that child, with wonder for the world. I am still that child, inquisitive and kind, who has done her best to survive with the tools she has had. I love her, every piece of her, every line of the circle, every loop.

When I feel lost, when I find myself slipping away, I draw out that same circle. I start in the center, with me. I remember, remind myself, of my core qualities. On the outer edge, I trace out my current struggles, and I draw an arrow from those hardships back to the center—remind myself that I can always return, that I am never far from my core, from my truth.

I do this now, pull a pad of paper out. I have been having a hard day and realize as I write that this could help me sort through some of my present challenges. Today, what lines my outer circle, my current hardship, is fear. Fear of the future, fear of the unknown. I trace back to the center of the circle and find a trait so important to me that I have written it down four times, a trait that comes to mind as I imagine a younger version of myself: gentle. Gentle, gentle, gentle. I can return to this. I can go toward my fear with a gentle curiosity.

Looking at this paper now, the circles that shape me, I am reminded of the concentric rings of a tree. Each ring, each year, has formed what it is now. Each tree that stands high above me was once as small as an acorn. Each of these trees has had a messy and complex past and will have a future of more of the same. And yet, in this one moment (and each other moment forevermore), each of these trees is exactly perfect, exactly as it is. If I honor the natural flow of life in all its forms, then I must also honor myself and the strange and perfect ways in which I have been able to grow.

I am always impressed by the manner in which trees are able to grow around obstacles. I love seeing trees that have formed around fences, ones that jut up and out of sidewalks and whose roots run through cement like butter. I love the trees that exist perched atop abandoned buildings and the trees growing sideways, upside down, all around. Trees each grow in unique, often perplexing ways, making do with what they have. This does not sully them. On the contrary, these utterly unique and often absurd growth patterns are what make trees so spectacular.

When I am consumed in shame over my past, when I am chastising myself for mistakes made during an earlier period of my life, I turn to the trees. I witness them, and in doing so, I am able to return to myself. I witness the trees, their brazenness, their willingness to stand, tall and naked, and say: *See all of me. Love me as I am.*

What would it look like to see myself in the same way that I see trees, to always marvel at my own resilience, my own ability to clear a path through the chaos of my life? What would it look like to honor the choices of a younger me, the scars in my skin and the pains in my heart, in the same way that I admire the patterns crafted out of a tree trunk forced to grow through metal? Would I laugh at myself for my ugly demarcations, or would I laugh with myself, gleefully noting that it is these exact marks that have allowed me to soar beyond them, to reach the heights where I live today?

I am beginning to see myself in this way. I am beginning to look with wonder upon all the circles within me. I am beginning to see we're not so different, the trees and I. I am beginning to see there is room enough in the soil for my roots, space in the sky for my branches to soar. I am beginning to see there is room for us all, even room for the parts of us we try to hide away. Let it all see the sunlight.

I am beginning to see that which I have always known: the trees are always here. The trees are always quiet, present. The trees are always pulling my feet into the ground, holding me steady. *Chi è qui?* I'll keep asking. Who is here?

I can ask this of the world around me, and I can ask it inside. When I feel ashamed or sad, angry, anxious, when I feel myself slipping away from my center in any capacity, I can ask of myself: *Chi è qui?* Which parts of me are present right now who need my attention, my love?

Just now, I feel myself growing sad, try to distract myself from it. No. No. Feel. I lay on my bed, thrash around, feel it. Feel the pain. I see. There is a part of me that is so afraid to be abandoned by those I love. There is another part of me that is so anxious about the future. There is another part of me, so small, who just wants to know everything is okay. I do not ignore these parts. I look at them, I see them. I do not try to rationalize their pain away. I understand. I witness. I hold them. I show them, I have my center. I am here.

We are never alone. We are all connected. Every part of us makes us whole. Each of us makes this forest.

I ask once more: *Chi è qui?* Now, in silence, let us see.

Sunflowers

THIS IS my last love letter to you. I don't know how I got here—writing about you in a book that's full of plants, full of family. You are not my family. You are not a plant, certainly. You are horrifyingly, breathtakingly, utterly: human. A human I used to know.

This is my last letter to you. You are here, you are here in my mind and on these pages, because of course you are. Because I cannot write a book about loss without writing about you. I cannot write about love without writing about you.

I write about you long after we finish speaking. I write and write. You are my favorite topic for a year, until I tire. I tire of thinking about someone who does not think of me. I tire of writing letters to nowhere.

I write about other things. I meet other people. Life moves on, in all the ways it always does. I do not think of you for a while. And then I am sitting, I am getting ready to write about sunflowers, and I realize that you are the person I want to share with. To write to, one last time. Let me show you what I have learned.

I plant sunflower seeds this spring because I am obsessed with the idea of something so big growing from something so small. I understand, theoretically, that all life works this way—that I too was once a single cell, that every living being begins as something we can hold balanced on the tip of a finger. I know this in theory, and yet there is something special about sunflowers, something about actually getting to see that little seed and watch it grow in real time. It feels as close as one can get to playing God. It is having a hand in creation. It is writing the story of the Earth.

I plant the seeds in a bed by our front door. They sprout in no time, and all summer long I watch them grow. They are mammoth sunflowers, meaning they can reach heights of up to twelve feet tall. I am diligent and protective over my sunflowers all season, watering them regularly and spraying with a repellent to protect against the woodland creatures that live in the area. Despite my love of these plants, there are stretches of time when I am not wary enough, and the deer come in for an attack. During the first round, after a heavy rain that washes away the putrid scent of the spray, they destroy two-thirds of the leaves. The plants look silly and barren and I consider ripping them all out, starting over. But they are three feet tall already and I am determined. I cut the plants back to the top leaf set and pray for the best.

The sunflowers show me, remind me, that life is resilience, that all life is creative and ingenious. The plants continue to grow, to flourish, with only small scars on their stems to show their past damage. Some of the plants split in two, dividing where they are cut and branching out—they become more than they were before the wound. The deer, a supposed menace, instead act as a positive mutative force.

All summer long, the sunflowers continue to grow, tall and ever-thickening stalks with leaves the size of my hand protruding out. All green, no flowers in sight. I wait patiently. The plants soon tower over me. I watch them each day as I leave the house and check in on them from my bedroom window above. A few of the smaller ones still get nibbled on occasionally, but most have now reached heights that are out of reach of any land bound critter. The sunflowers sway in the wind, and I watch them turn to face the sun. I can see them reaching toward her, soaking up the energy she provides. Phototropism—the response to the stimulus of sunshine. Sunflowers are the most obvious example of this feature, always turning toward the light, never abashed in their desire. I understand their love of sun—a desperate one, sickening, entirely one-sided. The sunflowers take, but they cannot give to the one they love. They have nothing that the sun needs.

Finally one morning I spy something new, something unusual, on the tallest of the plants. A bud. The first bud. The other plants soon follow suit, all budding up and then, suddenly, in bloom. To watch a sunflower head open, especially a mammoth one, is to marvel in the face of the sun itself. It does not seem real—these perfect yellow-orange petals unfurling, the hugeness of it, the grace of it. I stick my hand up to one in comparison (my hand fully stretched not reaching edge to edge) and snap a picture—I want to capture the size of it, the magnitude.

Then the bees. If ever there is reason to plant sunflowers it is for the pollinators, the sweet bees that arrive, hungry and vivacious. Watching them swarm each day is the greatest treat, knowing I have gifted them this food. Witnessing the symbiosis in action is a marvel—the sunflowers feed the bees and at the same time the bees pollinate the sunflowers. Without one the other would perish. This is how I once felt about you, that I could not go on in your absence. Or at least I did not want to. The reality is I have been without you for a long time now and am still solid, whole. My need for you was less essential, more contrived than that of the bees. I can make honey on my own.

The sunflowers only bloom for a week or so. All that growth, all that energy, for one performance. I learn that each sunflower head contains thousands of flowers, that the flowers are minuscule pieces of the entirety. This soothes me, this community of sunflowers clustered together, each patiently awaiting pollination as they sway as one in the breeze.

Over time the heads begin to droop. The bees have done their job, and the thousands of little sunflowers on each plant are busy turning themselves into seeds. These seeds grow heavy, and the weight of it pulls the heads toward the Earth. One day, during a particularly windy storm, the largest of the plants snaps in half, falling to the ground. I decide to take the rest of the plants down too, see that they are ready, weighted and tired.

I carefully saw the heads off of each, knowing that while the life cycles of these plants have been completed, there is still much work ahead for the little seeds that now protrude. I rub my hand back and forth across the seeds, loosening them. I spread them everywhere, thousands covering every bed of mulch in my front yard. I want the birds to have easy access. I want to return life to where it belongs. It is almost unbearably beautiful to be a part of the cycle of things, and it feels like a trick or cheat to get to participate so openly, so freely. I feel like I am being let in on a secret, the natural flow of the world. Is it really this easy to participate? This easy to remember how gorgeous it is to be alive?

Within weeks a majority of the seeds have disappeared, gobbled up by birds and chipmunks and any other creatures that come across them. Whichever seeds remain and can stay warm enough in clusters through the winter will germinate and sprout come spring. The true beauty of the sunflowers comes not from the impressive show they put on during the week or two they are in bloom—but rather, it's in all the life they spur. All the creatures they feed, all the seed children that will go on to grow their own massive stalks, all the carbon their leaves absorb.

There is beauty in the moment certainly, but the moment does not have to extend forever in order for its impact to. The lessons and joy of a single moment, a single blossom, a single relationship can extend onward forever in an endless cycle of love, of life, of a beauty without bound or judgment.

I grow sunflowers from seed because I want control. I want to take this small seed and shove it into the Earth and have it grow. When the sunflowers bloom I take a thousand pictures, just as I write about you a thousand times over, because I know both will not last, because I am desperate to capture the beauty. But a photo is not the same as a flower, and words are not the same as holding you. These things are replicas, and disappointing ones. But the truth is, they are unnecessary.

I do not need to hold onto the images of the sunflowers because they will be back next year, when the weather is warm and the soil is just right. I can cherish the fact that there are birds and bees with full tummies, fed by my desire to create a more loving planet. I grow sunflowers from seeds because to grow something is to tell the world: I love you. I am getting better at that—at loving freely, without expectation.

I am telling you about the sunflowers when what I really want to say is: I forgive you. You had your limitations, your capacity, and you loving me for an extended period was beyond the realm of possibility. I did not, could not, see that then. I see it now.

There are so many things I want to say to you here, though I know these words may never reach you (I know I will not send them). I want to say: I saw you in the sunflowers. I want to say: I saw our relationship play out in those giants. I want to say: I watched them grow and bloom, and I inhaled the grandness of it, and I finally understand that what we shared was never something that could last. That sometimes beauty must be fleeting in order to be beautiful at all. I want to say: sometimes beauty is not in the obvious moments, in the bright colors of a petal or the warmth of an embrace. Sometimes beauty is in absence, in twinges of the past, in memories, and in promises of a future that can be just as—even more—giving and gorgeous than that which we have already known.

I want to say: to know you at all was beautiful, was enough. I want to say: I wish I could have been present then, could have enjoyed the moment that our relationship was while it was happening instead of always reaching ahead, searching for more. I want to say: If I had been, present, it would not have gone the way it did, and it would not be life. I want to say: in that case, I don't take back a thing.

I want to say: what we had was good for having existed at all, and everything it gave me has become seeds again, replenishing the birds and the Earth and myself. The sunflowers are gone, but next year new ones will form. Our love, my love for you, is over, but that love created the seeds for new love, love that will awaken from dormancy and sprout forth when the conditions are right. Your love has taught me, given me, exactly what it was supposed to, and for that I am blessed. For that, I am better. I want to say: thank you for the moment, when I wanted a lifetime. I want to say: you deserve all the beautiful things in this world. I want to say: I know now that I do too.

Perennials

IN THE world of plants, to oversimplify everything, there are annuals, and there are perennials. Annuals live for a single growing season, one spring and one summer, and then die off. A perennial, on the other hand, can return year after year.

On the surface, perennials die back in the fall and winter just the same as annuals do. The leaves blacken and drop, and the plant begins to wilt and collapse. While for an annual this death is total and complete, the perennials are accustomed to the weather, have evolved to survive. Though these plants die back on the surface, the root system remains alive. The plant enters a period of dormancy, and the roots rest all winter long. Come spring, when the soil warms and the sun hits harder, the perennials will reemerge.

Some plants are annuals because they only have a single growing season in them. They flourish and bloom for a summer, produce seeds, drop the seeds, and that's that. Because their life cycle is so short, they are on a brief and ceaseless mission to reproduce, to create seeds. A single process, a whole lifetime, one season. With this mission and time crunch encoded in their DNA, they will put out flowers over and over again in the hopes of forming viable offspring. The showiness of these plants, their constant blooms, is for the attention of the bees and the butterflies, the occasional hummingbird, who will help in this process of pollination. We humans are grateful yet unintentional recipients of their beauty.

Other annuals are not annuals at all, have only become as much because of how we grow them. Some—many—annuals are in fact perennial elsewhere and can come back year after year in warmer climates. It is because we take these plants native to the tropics and other warm environments and bring them to our neck of the woods, our homes. They thrive in the warmth of the summer but come the cold of fall, these plants cannot survive. These southern perennials become annual when brought here, up north. Used to more mild winters, the harsh frosts and snows we have here are no match for their tender roots.

Determining where plants are perennial is based on hardiness. Different areas, different parts of the country, are delineated as different USDA hardiness zones. The zones range from 3a to 11b, with 3 indicating the coldest environment. Often perennials that are purchased at a nursery, like the one where I work, are labeled to indicate where they are hardy.

Here in Connecticut, we exist on the cusp of zones 6 and 7, and we can plant species that are hardy to these zones. I never understood this before, the native nature of plants. That some plants are from here, belong here, know how to survive the winters. I didn't understand.

I used to think that everything in our garden at home has always been there, has always been growing. I did not understand that once upon a time, someone planted all of it. Every inch. I thought the Earth acted alone and we just stumbled upon her. I never understood before, this human hand in the natural world. The entanglement of it all.

There is no doubt in my mind that I value perennials more than annuals. I think it is the lazy gardener in me—with perennials I can plant once and be done. Annuals require innovation year after year.

There is something lovely though, beyond the laziness it allows, of planting plants that are from here, that want to be here, that do well here. Plants that can get snug in the ground all winter, plants that want to return in the spring. It's nice to work with the Earth, to add to her, to know it will last. I am trying to create something that will last. Or at least something that will extend.

I want my life to be beautiful. I want to be beautiful. I want to matter. I want people to love me, because I exude beauty and because I am kind, because I am good. So much of creation is about avoiding death. I am doing it right here, with these words. I am building bridges with sentences and praying that they will last beyond me. Hoping, despite myself, despite what I know, that creating something that can live beyond me will somehow extend my life as well. At least extend the impact.

I want my life to be one that leaves the Earth a more beautiful place. I am afraid sometimes, when I am cranky and mean or tired and rude, that I have failed. That I am failing. The truth is though, the beauty is in trying. The beauty is in saying: I will do better tomorrow. I will do better right now. The beauty is in saying: wherever I am at, whoever I am in this moment, right here, right now, that is enough, and that is right. The love of beauty, the attempt to create beauty, the understanding that it is all already beautiful, is the beauty of it all.

I create with words and I create with dance and now I create with plants. I did not know that plants could be creative, and I feel ridiculous now for saying as much. They are works of art come to life. They are the most gorgeous, the most variant and giving alive things I have ever known.

I am writing these words to leave something beautiful behind, something beautiful for you to see, to hold and read. These words are for anyone who stumbles upon them.

I have decided to return to Italy. It is mid-July when I realize I want to go back, but not yet, knowing that I want to stick around to watch the seasons change, to see summer fade to fall fade to winter. I tentatively decide on February to go back. It feels symbolic, to have come home for a full year. Four seasons. A complete loop around the calendar.

In my mind's eye I have always pictured the year in a particular way. I see a calendar year as blocks of black and white, linked in a circle. January a white square, connected to February as a black square, and so on and so on, finally connecting a black December back to white January. A circle, a loop, around and around we go. In my mind time has never been moving forward, just around and around and around.

I see the process of healing in the same way. Not as a straight line—from acknowledging I am not okay to I am okay. But as a sort of loop-di-loop, growing and healing and struggling and suffering and growing and healing some more, around and around, always moving and progressing but never in a linear way, never straightforward.

It is hard to remember this, in those moments when everything feels dark, that this is healing too. I think healing is always happening, and if we can remember this, all life can be beautiful. I am always re-remembering. In moments where I become flustered, sad, scared, I ask myself: What can this teach me? How can this experience help me to grow? It is all healing if we let it be. It is all beauty if we say so. I say so.

I will ride the loop and circle of time and healing back to Italy. I am here and soon I will be there. Maybe one day I will be back here. I am riding the circles, I am spinning, I am floating, I am free.

I decide to return to Italy after a year at home because I miss it, because part of my heart lives there and I want to go back to find it. Because I finally want to become fluent in the language that I love so much, a language that speaks to me in the same way plants speak to me—where I can love it and admire it and yet know I am still outside of it, not quite grasping, not quite understanding. I want to understand.

I find an apartment in Rome, one just outside of Vatican City. I find an intensive Italian language course, where I will be studying the language all day every day. It is a plan, and it is perfect, and the death is behind us. I see life ahead, I see a future, a family in the hills of Italia. One of my own.

Before I return, I know I need to leave something behind.

I know I need to create something that can live here, here in Connecticut, here on this continent, here on this patch of land that I have come to know and to love. It is why I am writing these words, here. I am writing right now to leave a bit of my love in this language behind. I am writing right now to try to create beauty with words. I am succeeding, even if the only person who finds these words beautiful is me. I have decided that that is enough. That is, in fact, everything. To love myself so deeply, finally, that that love compounds itself, multiplies, fills me. Till I am only love, till it is impossible to do anything but find beauty in my own existence, in my own ideas.

I write these words and I plant perennials. In a moment of epiphany, I realize that even when I am gone, I can have something here. I can leave a piece of me, a part of my heart, in the roots of plants. I am planting perennials to leave something beautiful at my home. These are just for my mom and dad.

I never thought I would have a good relationship with my parents. Was never sure I wanted one. I grew up feeling so alienated from my family, so distrustful of the whole group. I never expected to be where I am today: to think of leaving them and have tears well in my eyes. I never expected I would miss them. I miss them already.

The project of planning which perennials to plant is made easier by the nature of my work. Every day at my job I get to explore plants, discover ones I never knew, learn which ones are best suited to different lighting conditions, soil conditions, et cetera. I spend more time than usual hovering by the perennials at work, making decisions, figuring out where to weave new roots.

On one of my days off, I go over to the garden center. I purchase a few plants for the shade and head home. I begin planting, and as I do so the sky opens up, it begins to pour. A past version of myself would have immediately run inside, would have hid from the rain. But a past version of myself would never have been planting anything in the first place. A past version of myself would have never understood—I am one with the Earth. I am always okay in her arms, even in the rain.

So I stay, and let the rain fall. I dig large holes in the ground, fill them with plants. I watch as the rain feeds them, nurtures them. The immediacy of Mother Nature is a marvel. And I am a part of that. I have to remind myself all the time—I am a part of this. This natural world. And not just in a superficial way, where I can see it and touch it and admire it. But really truly a part of. As in—I came from this. As in we all came from this. As in—we build up our lives with structure and borders and systems and categories. We keep everything nice and tidy and neat. We do all this and we forget, we lose sight of the fact that we are still animals, still part of that kingdom of creatures. We are still alive. We are still dying. To be human is to be separate. To remember, to be alive, is to return to the Earth. The good thing is, we can always return.

I continue planting more perennials throughout the summer and into early fall. Each one that I plant feels like a hug, from me now to my mother and father in the spring. I want them to see the fresh blooms that I have staggered throughout the season, and I want them to know: we are so loved by our creation.

I learn at work that there has been a push in recent years to plant more native plants. Customers regularly ask us to point them in the direction of natives. While some don't always understand exactly what this means, the impetus and trend is a good one. It is a return.

To plant native plants means to plant something that grows here naturally, as opposed to a plant that has been brought in, that is found elsewhere. The reasoning behind this is to work with, rather than against, the natural world. We are in it. We are it. Let us not fight ourselves any longer.

Native plants are ones that the local bees and hummingbirds and butterflies are already used to. These pollinators and the other creatures of the world feast on plants, and they are able to do so with greater ease when they are surrounded by ones they know.

I am terrified of losing the bees. I am terrified that they are dying off. Planting perennials is a gift of love to my parents and to the natural world. It is saying: I see you, I see your ache. I ache too. I ache with you. Let us heal together. Let us bring all the healing back home.

This summer after existing for twenty-five years without ever being stung by a bee, I finally break my lifelong streak. I am cleaning the pansies and chatting with a landscaper at the garden center when I feel a prick, a sting. I watch the bee fall, see the slight red welt on my wrist. I am not hurt, though I am saddened. Another loss of life, this time by my unwitting hand. I plant a salvia to repent.

I set out to make a list of all the perennials I put into the ground this year. I trace around the garden, mentally mapping out everything new and growing, all the green I have inserted. I want to put down on paper that which is already in the soil. I want to be able to hold all of it in my hand all at once.

Over the course of this season, I have planted two astilbes, both "Vision in Red," three Japanese anemones, all white, one cardinal flower in purple, one ligularia, three brunnera of the "Jack Frost" variety, and three white salvias, specific varieties unknown (forgotten).

Despite the plethora of plants I have added to our yard, part of me still wishes I had done more, filled more spaces. I want to cover every inch of soil in green. My biggest regret is not planting a bleeding heart in the shade. A bleeding heart looks exactly as it sounds, a stunning perennial with flowers that drip in a heart shape so true I am certain that this is the originator of the word, of the idea. Mother Nature is giving with both hands to everything, all the time. To us all.

I keep thinking about planting one, a bleeding heart, but I never do. I still do not know why. But maybe the answer is as simple as the fact that not everything can be planted in a single season. That to plant something takes time and energy, and it is time and energy that I do not have—by merit of the fact that I want to do it, and do not. I cannot plant everything I want to and that is enough. I will not say everything here in these pages that I want to, and that will be enough, too. Would I forsake all the perennials in my garden because I am one short?

I feel ashamed sometimes for all the times I have had to rest, to slow. I love that perennials go dormant in the winter. I love that a period of rest is part of their existence, their way of being. Integral to their growth.

I, like the perennials, have had many periods of rest in my life. Periods of dormancy. During these periods I felt pathetic, absurd. Looking back—I am so grateful to myself. So grateful for the rest. That I was able to rest at all.

I want to slow down. It is why I love plants, because they exist on a slower plane. A completely different mode of being. They have learned to grow and move in a way that is so different from us. They grow with a patience I attempt to embody. They grow in a way that says: my body knows where I will go next and there is nothing I need to rush. I want to understand this way of being. I am beginning to understand. This is the beginning, every moment.

My friend Anna comes to visit me in Connecticut one weekend, takes the train in from the city. We go for a walk in the woods across the street from my house, and we talk about the plants and the trees and what it means to be alive. I explain to her, here in this forest of my childhood and now my adulthood, a forest that will live beyond me and all of us and that we will all be a part of one day, in some way, I explain to her here the beauty of perennials.

I point out the giant ferns that line the walking path in the woods. Ferns have been around for ages, prehistoric creatures that have felt and lived through a changing planet. They are living fossils, and you can sense it when you look at them. Ah yes, this is something the dinosaurs marveled at too. It all makes sense. I cannot explain this. Some felt things we only know in our bodies, not with words.

I point out the giant ferns as an example of a perennial. I explain:

these ferns are so giant because they are old. I show her a smaller one: this here will be just as large as the others one day. They grow and grow all summer long, and then in the fall they brown, and the leaves die. The root system stays underground, waiting, resting, ready to reemerge and grow some more when the weather warms.

I can't stop thinking about that—the essential nature of rest. We humans, animals, do it each night. We lay our bodies down, shut our eyes, and sleep. Our bodies have a chance to recover, our minds have a moment to process the day prior, everything falls into place. To rest is to heal, to rest is to grow.

I show Anna the ferns and the forest because I want everyone I love to understand: you are a part of something so beautiful. These plants are here to hold you. It is okay to rest, and it is okay to breathe. We are all a part of the natural flow of the world, and I want to bring us all back to that. I want us to return.

For a while I am not certain that I want to go back to Italy at all. The day I get the job offer at the garden center I cry to my mom. She does not think I will want the job because I have spoken of returning to Italy soon. I want the job because I know I need to stay. I tell her: *I am so afraid.* I tell her: *I am so afraid that if I leave, if I am not here, with you, with our family, then you and Dad are going to die.*

I know this fear is irrational. I know that in my bones. But it's also not irrational. There is truth to the imminence of death, of the death of all those I love. Every single I person I love I will lose. I will lose my mom and my dad. I will lose my friends. And if I do not witness their deaths, if I am not around to see them go, it will only be because these people have lost me first.

I know this, that everyone dies, that death is imminent, that death is the most natural part of life. The most essential part. But I am still afraid. I am afraid that if I loosen my grip, if I fly away, go back to Italy, if I let my sights off my family, then I will lose it all. I am trying to let the plants show me the way. I am trying to let the plants guide me through the fear.

One of the perennials I plant, the cardinal flower, is a relatively short-lived perennial. Whereas some perennials, like hydrangeas and rhododendrons, are known to live for decades, even a century or more, other perennials exist on the opposite end of the spectrum and only live for a handful of years. The cardinal flower is one such plant, lasting about four years on average.

The magic of the cardinal flower is that even though an individual plant will die after a few loops around the calendar, the plant will consistently reseed itself, creating new plants year after year. Multiplying, filling the space, over and over. One plant is lost in the shuffle, but it is always replaced. There is never a lack of purple, despite the death. There is never a lack of purple, because death makes room for life.

I plant only one cardinal flower even though I want the soil to be full. I figure, let the plant fill the space as it pleases. Let it place its seeds and children where it may. Though its life may be shorter than some, it is its own, and it is beautiful.

Let my parents watch their beauty multiply. Let them feel joy in their hearts as they do.

I am going back to Italy because I want to, because some part of me needs to, because it is my journey (because I say so). I am going back not because I am unafraid, but because I am—so afraid. I am terrified of death and I am terrified of loss and that is gorgeous—to feel so much, to feel it all. That's the beauty. To feel afraid and say: yes, and. Yes, I am afraid, and I will go anyway. Yes, loss scares me, and I will face it head on. Yes, I still have so much to learn, so many lessons ahead, so much I do not know, and I am ready. I am here. I am here and breathing and alive.

A perennial is a plant that has made its home in the soil. It has gotten cozy in there. I have gotten so cozy here, too. I feel rooted. I feel like maybe I too could spend a couple loops around the calendar here, could see what sort of growth permanency allows.

I remember that despite my love of them, I am not a plant. And my roots are less fixed, and my body can transplant myself as I please. I am free to roam.

I picture myself in Italy in a few months, immersed in the

language, meeting new people, eating too much pasta. I smile just thinking about it. I know I'm on the way, on the right path. I know the plants will carry me there.

I am scared to leave a home I have come to love with my whole heart, and I also know I will never truly leave it. My hands placed each salvia, each astilbe and brunnera, into the ground. My handiwork is henceforth tethered in the soil. I am not a plant, but I am one with the plants, and I am always home.

Propagation

I⊤ is my mother who teaches me what a gift it is to give plants. What a gift it is to oneself, to the world, to the people we love. She has been teaching me this for years, for a lifetime, though it is only recently that I can see this, this gift she has given me.

My mother, self-admittedly, does not know as much about plants as I do. She tells me that I have learned more about plants in one year than she has in a lifetime. I believe this to be true. What she does know about, perhaps more than myself, is care. She knows how to show the people she loves exactly how she feels.

My mother and I did not always get along well, particularly in my teenage years. There used to be such a wall up between us, a block that I felt I could not get beyond. I remember one day, standing in our family room, facing her. Feeling desperately sad, wanting her to comfort me, and feeling as though there were a physical barrier between us, something blocking her from seeing me, for loving me as I was. As I am.

This block, this barrier, has come down over the years. Not through any magic nor any one moment, but rather through a continuous desire on both our parts to improve our communication, to understand the other better. The saving grace has been my ability to understand my mother not just as the woman who birthed and raised me, but as a full and complex human, someone with a life before me and a life outside of me. When I see her as she is, as her whole self, I feel only love.

My mother, like her mother before her, loves and understands beauty. She loves the breathtaking visions of the world. And so, despite a purported lack of knowledge on the subject, she has always been skilled at saying *I love you* with plants.

For years before she died my grandmother was housebound, did not go further than her porch save for the occasional doctor's appointment. She was confined. My mother decided: I will create beauty within these boundaries of living.

Every year for Mother's Day, my mother planted. She bought sweet potato vines and geraniums, coleus and petunias, and she planted. She filled the pots on my grandparents' porch, infused them with flowers and greens and life.

Each summer it became my grandfather's job to water everything, a task he took quite seriously. Every day he filled a jug with water and poured it upon the plants until they had their fill. He wanted to keep the beauty alive, for his bride, for his bees. My mother gifted plants, and she gifted purpose.

Besides planting for my grandparents each year, my mother shows her love with flower arrangements. She has done this always, for everyone—to celebrate, to mourn, to honor, to love. While I am still living in Venice, I receive a massive bouquet of white lilies at the house one day. She sends them a week before Christmas, simply because she wants me to have something beautiful for the holidays. *I love you, I love you, I love you,* she says with each stem.

When the flowers arrive at the door I am overwhelmed by their beauty, filled by her love. I imagine her on the phone with the florist in Venice, painstakingly ensuring they have all my information, that I will receive my lilies promptly. My mother is nothing if not determined in her quest to make the lives of those she loves more beautiful, even fleetingly so.

On any occasion, my mother knows there is nothing quite like receiving—and nothing quite like giving—something living, something green or floral. No better way to say I care. While I am working at the garden center, she asks me to place an order so she can send an arrangement to one of her friends who has had a particularly hard week. She describes the arrangement to me: compact, cube vase, all white. All white because that was my grandmother's favorite color of flowers. Dede's love of white petals is inherited by my mother immediately after her passing. Perhaps this is a language of love passed down matrilineally in my family. Perhaps plants are something each woman in my line comes to in her own way, when she is ready.

Perhaps then it is only natural that I fall into plants—headfirst, head over heels. Passionately. Love at first sight. It becomes the way I understand the rhythm of the world and my place within it. I learn how vulnerable and at peace I can feel in the garden, how at home I feel with dirt under my nails.

I cherish my time spent in the garden, working with the ground. There is something innate in being a human playing in the soil. Whenever I get my trowel and shears out, I know I am tapping into that which is completely natural, an activity that millennia of humans have experienced before me. This tender caretaking of the Earth. I revere it, honor it. I love it, and at the same time—I hope it is not blasphemous to say—it does not compare to the intimacy and wonder I experience with the plants I get to take inside, make members of my home.

My mother tells me that Dede was like this too, though to a greater extreme. Not one for getting her hands dirty outside, she was never much of a gardener. Yet she would always, religiously, bring the outside in, keeping something green inside at all times. I see this now looking at old photographs of her—trails of ivy poking out of pots on a bookshelf, or a planted pothos pooling off a coffee table.

My father shares with me that his mom, a woman whose first name I bear as my middle but never met before she passed, was similar to Dede. No gardener, but a lover of houseplants. He tells me this while I attempt to grow an avocado tree from seed (I do not succeed). My father notes that his mom used to do this too—prick toothpicks into the seed of the fruit and suspend it over standing water. I am intrigued that both my grandmothers did not play in the garden yet wanted their homes to be shrouded in green. My genes have come together to help me bring the Earth inside.

We humans create shelter to keep the elements out, to stay safe from the weather, and to hide from offensive creatures and bugs. We build walls around ourselves and pretend that we are separate from nature. What sweet irony then, what fairytale trickery, that plants manage to find their way in. They are just that beautiful, we want them that much, that we allow them to blur the carefully constructed boundaries between the natural world and our own. We pull plants in, and they pull us out.

Thinking now about the plants that currently live in my home paints a soft smile on my face, and I let out an easy sigh. I am so touched by their presence, held by them all. It can be easy to forget that plants are alive. Often, they are treated as works of art, as adornment, as opposed to something breathing and growing. I admit that I used to see them this way: stagnant, immobile. Decorative. Now, I have become too intimate with them to forget that they are just as alive as I am. That they shift and grow alongside me. There is reassurance in having so much life around me, so many breathing creatures in my home.

The first of my houseplants, and now the largest, is aloe vera. This is a plant I have had for years and one that grows and reproduces itself repeatedly. This is where my love of propagation begins, where my mother's teachings extend. This is how I come to see the beauty in gifting the growing green goodness of the world.

Merriam-Webster states that the technical definition of "propagate" is: "to produce (a new plant)." There is sweet simplicity in such a sentiment. To propagate is to take one plant and create many. What Merriam-Webster does not reveal is that propagation is an addiction, and a devotion, and pure magic distilled in earthly forms.

Aloe is an especially lovely plant to propagate, simply because it does so much of the work for you. The lazy lady's propagative plant, if you will. The main mature plant is known as the mother, which puts out new plants—pups—around herself. These pups, connected to the mother via the root system, can grow into plants of their own if given proper encouragement. For the last few years, I take it upon myself to forge a new path for the baby aloes, removing them from the mother and giving them their own pots to grow in.

I've developed quite the collection of aloes over the years. I cannot keep up with the speed at which the plants multiply, and soon the planters take over an entire hallway. I realize it is time to share, it is time to let go, it is time for some of these beauties to spread their wings, leave home. It is time.

I gift the first of these aloes to a close friend, a fellow plant obsessive who I know it will be safe with. I pass along this plant, and something shifts. I realize that I now feel a stronger connection to this person, a cord linking us, something holding us together that did not exist before. There is a divine presence in the gifting of this aloe. Indescribable joy, love, in knowing that the daughter plant lives in her bedroom while the mother is here with me. We are held together, a firm whisper of plant energy between us.

The floodgates open after this, and I want to feel this connection with everyone I know. I gift other aloe pups to other friends and am amazed over and over again by the deepening of my love for these people. It is because I am learning, repeatedly, that we are all already connected. The gifting of the plants makes that which is already naturally present, obvious. We are one, all taking care of each other, growing alongside one another on this abundant Earth.

I feel absurd sometimes when I try to talk about that. That one-ness that I believe is real, that we can all tap into. I feel absurd when I try to articulate it to other people, that I see myself not as a separate entity, not as a self, but as one small part of a grander whole. I see myself, I see all of us—every person, every plant, every living thing—as the universe animated, the universe chatting with herself in different forms, learning about herself. What are we doing here anyway if not learning? Who am I, what am I, if not stardust, dancing and playing in this beautiful body of mine for a blink in time before that same stardust is folded into other beings, other beauty?

The process of propagation is one I adore, one that I look forward to immensely. This spring I wait eagerly for the weather to warm enough to bring my aloes outside. Once the last frost has passed, I carry them out into the sunshine one by one. I set up a large tarp over the table on our patio and get to work.

There are several plants that need propagating. The mother plant, the eldest, has five small pups growing beside her that I plan to remove. Another midsize aloe that I propagated a few years ago also has an offshoot, and I will repot this one as well. I gather my materials: all the new terra cotta pots, recently purchased from the garden center, my soil (a huge bag of regular potting mix as well as several small bags of cactus/succulent soil), coffee filters for drainage, and shears.

I begin with the mother plant. I lay the pot on its side, work my hands into the soil. I like to propagate my aloes when the soil is dry—the Earth slides out a bit easier, cannot grasp the edges of the pot quite as well as when moisture is present. I gently pull the mass of soil and plants out, paying careful attention to the smallest of the pups, the most vulnerable among them.

I loosen the root ball, working my fingers into the soil, teasing dirt from plant. I am consistently gobsmacked by the size of the mother plant. She is massive from the ground up, her leaves huge and thick after six years of growth. Seeing the totality of her, roots and all, only adds to the wonder. Her roots are hefty, intricate, and plentiful, and I am so honored to witness her, so blessed to hold all of her life, all that she is, in my two hands.

Some of the pups come apart from the mother easily, with little more than a gentle pull. A few of the others are more attached, still securely tethered to their creator. It is for these that my shears come in handy, and I clip the root system between mother and child. A break to bear new life.

I prepare the planters. I line the bottom of each with a coffee filter, so that the water may drain through easily while the soil stays contained. I then proceed to fill the pots with a combination of the two types of potting soil I have procured: the regular mix, to help hold some water, combined with cactus soil, to ensure the water drains through with ease, does not overstay its welcome and rot the plants.

Once the pots are mostly full, I place the plants into their new homes. A planter for each, a space of their own. I stand them upright and tuck soil in around them, packing it in around the small roots just tightly enough to hold them but not so tightly that they are smothered by it.

When it comes time to repot the mother, I call to my father, ask for his hands. He obliges, holds the huge aloe up as I work the soil in around her massive roots. I am tinged with sadness as the soil falls in around her, knowing that it will be at least another year until I can once again marvel at all of her, can see with my own eyes that which is usually hidden underground.

I complete the planting process, arrange the pots on the ground, and stand facing my little family of aloes, utterly mesmerized. Propagation is a process of transfiguration. It is growth. It is giving into hope, saying: *I trust that you can grow on your own now. I trust in your capacity, your strength.*

A few of these plants are still at home with me today. Two others did not survive the hot summer sun and burnt up. A tragedy and a lesson—shade can be a welcome balm. The rest of the plants have been given away—to an aunt, to friends. I get pictures of these babies from time to time and am always thankful to witness their growth. I am touched to know that others care for that which I love.

This summer a friend of mine, someone I have gifted an aloe to, becomes curious about the propagation process. I tell her I will send a brief video explaining, and I do, except it is not brief. It clocks in at around thirty minutes, unintentionally. What begins as a simple explanation of a technical process quickly becomes a love story, a myth, a tale of the wonders and joys of propagating. It is a love story because to propagate is to tell the Earth, to tell ourselves, I want more. More beauty, more of you. Let us all be so lucky.

Propagation begins out of necessity for me, with my plethora of aloes. It becomes, almost immediately, something desperate. I need to gift plants to everyone I know, everyone I love. I need everyone to love plants as much as I do. I need everyone to know how much I love them.

To give a plant is to say I love you in what I believe is the purest way. It says, here, have something beautiful. It says, here, you deserve something in your home that will help you breathe better, will clean the air for you. It says, here, take this piece of my heart and nurture it, and let it nurture you.

At home, I begin almost exclusively growing plants that are easily propagated, and therefore easily gifted. I want to create a limitless supply of love on every windowsill, in every corner. While it is possible to propagate many plants via cuttings—taking a leaf or stem from a plant and rooting it in water or soil—I seek out plants that self-propagate, that show me when they are ready to reproduce themselves.

One of the most bountiful plants I bring home from work one day (being a plant lover working at a nursery is bad for the wallet, and good for the soul) is a pilea peperomioides, a member of the genus peperomia. The pilea is nicknamed the friendship plant, or the sharing plant, and both names are apt. A fast grower, it regularly produces babies around itself once it has reached maturity, babies that can be repotted and shared with ease.

The pilea is a peppy plant. Long petioles connect almost perfectly circular leaves to the stem. The leaves are open, playful, and the whole plant dances when you give the pot a shake. My mother begins lovingly referring to this as the "boing boing plant," her nickname mimicking the bouncing movements it makes when I carry it downstairs for water.

The pilea, the sharing plant, the boing boing, grows rapidly and fully. Since bringing it home just a few months ago, it has put out seven baby plants. All of these I have carefully removed, repotted, and gifted. Several went to friends, two to extended family, one to our neighbors. Each time I gift one I explain: *When your plant is mature, you can propagate it, too. You don't have to, but the possibility is there.* I am always praying that the love I share can multiply, can spread.

Another easily propagated plant I bring home is sedeveria Letizia. Sedeveria is a cross between two types of succulents: sedum, and echeveria. Sedum are perennial succulents, often grown as drought-tolerant crops that flower gorgeously. Echeveria are usually kept inside as houseplants. They have a lovely rosette shape, pleasing to the eye, and plump leaves, pleasing to the touch. Sedeveria is a hybrid of these two. Sedeveria Letizia does a particularly beautiful job of combining the best of these genera, possessing the capacity for flowering of the sedum, and the majestic rosette pattern of echeveria. It is a wonder.

I bring three of these home with me and leave them outside all summer. They flower continuously throughout the season, and their edges become tinged red by the gentle kiss of the sun. These small stunners explode in the sunshine, growing more rapidly than any succulent I have ever witnessed. By summer's end each of the three plants have multiplied themselves countless times over, and the planters are full of offshoots.

When the weather has cooled and it is time to bring the plants inside for the season, I feel the urge to share. To once again spread the love, spread the joy that these plants have already given me. I delight in the project. I bring the sedeveria into the kitchen, place a plastic tray on the marble island. I remove all three plants from their pots and get to work, cutting off baby plants from the mother. It is an extended process, and when it is complete a galaxy of new plants lies before me. I let them sit out overnight so the wounds can callous, and then I pot them all in small planters, the largest by themselves and the small ones in clusters of three.

The sedeveria root almost instantaneously, not uncommon in succulent propagation. While I love propagating any plant I can get my hands on, succulents hold a special place in my heart for the magic they perform. These plants struggle to reproduce themselves via pollination, and even when they are able to produce seeds, they are not always prosperous. Thus, many succulents have evolved to reproduce asexually, and brilliantly so. These plants know on a molecular level that their only chance of reproduction may be when a piece of themselves breaks and falls to the ground, and so they have learned to root quickly, and with vigor. They excel at this form of reproduction, cloning themselves over again in order to keep their species alive. Propagating them is therefore a breeze, a treat.

After the plants have rooted, I plot out in my mind who to gift them to. I am always thinking about plants, thinking about giving plants away. It is how I keep life in perspective, how I keep myself on a steady plane. When the world feels like it is falling to pieces, when nothing makes sense, there is nothing like honoring the simplicity of a plant and the enormity it represents. Nothing quite like saying: today I choose to share this simple piece of present peace. Today I choose to share love, with leaves.

Another plant I procure with the intent to propagate is a string of pearls. This exquisite succulent looks exactly as its name suggests, a collection of pearl-like green beads that elegantly cascade down the side of the pot. This plant is by far the easiest of all of mine to propagate. One can simply clip a small section of the pearls, place it on top of potting soil, and in several weeks the cutting will begin to root. I play with this plant ad nauseam, pruning and placing new pieces, creating baby plants that fill every crevice of the house. I begin to gift these, too.

A dear friend of mine moves into a new apartment this summer, a beautiful one-bedroom in the East Village. She mentions that she is looking to fill her space with plants. I know this is not a request, nor invitation, and yet I cannot help myself. When I go into the city for a visit, I pack a shopping bag full of each kind of easily propagated plant I possess: an aloe, a pilea, a sedeveria Letizia, and a string of pearls. I write her thorough instructions for each, explain their watering needs, ideal lighting conditions, and, of course, information on how to propagate them once they have reached maturity.

It is this friend of mine who helps inspire this book, opens up the possibility for it. Glancing through my care instructions, she notes that there is pleasure in reading my words, something special to be gleaned from the way I discuss these green beings. This notion brings me great joy, and I realize: this is all I want to do. Play with plants and write about plants. I realize: this can be a form of propagation too. Sharing my love with words, spreading the serenity plants bring through the very idea of them. Forming more connections, bridging more gaps.

I continue to use propagation to create ties between myself and the people I love. I attempt something somewhat covert, too, and decide to create a tie between two other people. I decide to utilize the power of plants for healing, curious about what is possible within the realm of propagation.

I have two friends, two people I am closer to than almost anyone else in the world. These friends of mine were once friends with each other, too. In fact, I became friends with one through the introduction of the other. Over the years, my friendship with both these wonderful women blossoms, while the friendship between the two of them comes to a shuddering halt. This division between two humans I love breaks my heart.

For ages I feel hopeless, certain that no reconciliation is possible. I know that these former friends love each other still, can sense it in the way they each speak about the other. And yet I do not know how to bridge the gap, cannot see a path forward through the hurt.

And so, I turn to the one idea that has never failed me, the gift that keeps on giving: propagation. I gift each of these women plants, ones that stem from the same origins. I divide my plants, pot them up, and pass them along. Siblings to share, unbeknownst to the other. Gifting from within the same family, completing a circle of care.

These two friends of mine now each possess a pilea from the same mother, and a sedeveria from the same mother, too. It is my hope, perhaps a fruitless one, that by linking them in this way, by having them tend to these plant sisters, a cord of healing will grow between them. A hug of plant energy, a line of love.

Writing this now, I know both of these women will one day read these words, will come to understand what I have done. I hope they know that these plants were gifted with love and without expectation. Gifted with only the hope (a hope that I have seen come alive with my own eyes): Plants can heal us all.

I see propagation as something that we do with plants, but also something that we do all the time, simply by existing. Every moment we propagate pieces of ourselves, parts of us that can root into the Earth and into the people we know and love, or even those we do not. A single conversation with a stranger may gift them the knowledge they need to make a positive shift in their life. A single moment of oneself, gifted to nature, can change everything. Can produce growth we never dreamed of.

I send a message to a friend recently, thanking him for existing, thanking him for being a part of my life. I thank him for sharing his creative and thoughtful mind with me. I send him this message because I want him to know that it was a conversation we had this summer that spurred my decision to return to Italy, to commit to studying the language full-time. I want him to know the impact he had on me, the way his presence alone, his way of being, completely shifted the trajectory of my life. I want him to know that he has propagated something beautiful simply by being.

When you propagate a plant, you are cloning the original, recreating it. However, despite the overlapping genetic code, this plant will become its own entity. It will create new growth patterns, develop into a wholly distinct creature. The baby comes from the mother, but becomes something else entirely. It is this notion of creation and separation that I consider when I think about becoming a mother.

Over the last several years I have put endless energy into healing myself. Healing from childhood and adulthood trauma, learning to be more compassionate and loving, tending to the garden of my body, of my mind. I have replenished and revitalized that which was lacking, and created beauty within myself that I never thought possible. I have become the person I never knew I could be, the human I did not dare imagine. Now, knowing who I am today, I feel ready to bring life into this world. I am ready, I am eager, to be a mother.

I seek to place a piece of myself, of my body and blood, out into nature, and I want to watch it grow. I understand that this piece of myself will not be me. Like the baby plants, my child will be an entirely different person, an existence complete unto themselves. I want to see what a part of me that is not me can become, knowing, hoping, that because of my healing, because of the care I will give to this being, they will exist beyond the realm of my own limitations.

My hope in having children is that they will be more loving than I am, than my mother is, than her mother was before her. My hope is that as we propagate, as we procreate, we take the best of ourselves, of our plants, of our souls, and we nurture them and allow them to become whoever they are meant to be. My hope is that to create life in any form is an act of love. Take this plant and breathe better. Take this plant, nurture it, and give it to those you love. Take this plant and know you are inextricably a part of a wondrous world. Take this piece of me, child of mine, and do with it what you will, however your heart guides you.

I will keep gifting plants for the rest of my life. I will propagate and fill every corner of my home with green, whether that is here or in Italy or somewhere else entirely. I will never stop trying to create beauty from beauty, life from life. I will never stop marveling at it either, the simplicity of creating something new, something breathing and whole and alive. I will always be touched by the power of plants, of propagation, of the connection they allow for.

My hope, my deepest desire, is that with these words you may also find beauty in the green things of this world, may also choose to multiply and spread the love. May you cultivate beauty and breath everywhere you turn. May every moment be an opportunity for growth. May your home be a sanctuary for life and for love. It is what you deserve.

We give pieces of ourselves, of the plants we love, and we do not know what will come of them. We cannot say with certainty how they will grow. All we can do is continue to hope, to trust that nature will run its course in exactly the way it is meant to. All we can do is lead with beauty, with love, and choose to show care. Choose vulnerability and passion, abandon all pretense, and give. When we allow ourselves to give freely, to be wholly ourselves, our love can root, and it can grow—perhaps into something more marvelous than anything or anyone that has come before.

Cut Flowers

ONE DAY I ask: What qualifies a flower as dead?

I am thinking about the florists' corner at work. A simple wooden counter. A double-basin sink. One long refrigerator full of flowers and a walk-in cooler full, too. A long hallway connected to the cooler filled with glass vases of every size and design.

I am thinking about the magic that happens over there, the art our florists create with petals, and I wonder: where is the line between life and death in the world of flowers?

Flowers are cut from their life source, their roots, and are transported around the globe. The cut flower trade is a fascinating one, and I find myself inquiring endlessly about shipping procedures. I am so curious: how is one able to cut off a living being's heart and lungs and have it still stand tall? (Cold.)

I receive the call that Dede has died a little after midnight. I head over to the house immediately. I do not remember who drives me, do not remember when I arrive there. I only remember knowing that I must go. Must say goodbye, to the body who brought so much beauty to my life.

I walk into Dede's bedroom and am flooded with sadness, as well as an intense appreciation for the immediacy of death's hold. Her skin has already begun to take on a waxy sheen and her body has a taught, rigid appearance which I have never witnessed— Dede, even in illness, always possessed a fluidity and physical grace about her. I see her body now, and there is no mistaking:

her life cycle is complete.

I love the smell of cut flowers at work. I experience this most fragrantly when I volunteer to remove the compost from the florists' corner. I walk the huge green bin out of the corner, through the greenhouses, all the way outside to the giant compost heap. It is here, dumping all the cut stems and leaves and excess petals, pulling out pounds of green weight, that the smell washes over me. With the smell, inevitable memories follow. This is the real joy.

The memories that appear in my mind's eye are of ballet performances, particularly after I had gone on stage. Standing outside with the whole extended family, taking photos with everyone. Everyone shoving flowers in my arms. Dede, standing to the side, so proud of her little ballerina. She came to every performance, always with flowers in hand.

There is such a particular scent to cut flowers, one that they all possess, regardless of the flavor of the petals. It is a smell not unlike that of fresh cut grass. It is an opening, water mixed with green death. To hold a cut flower in one's arms is a ceremony. What beauty in these corpses.

In the flower business, we do not use harsh words like "death." Instead, flowers are "fresh cut," which is technically true. I am curious why we draw away from even the notion of death. Why do we find such ghastliness in even the word itself, the very idea of the thing? (Fear.)

At Dede's after she dies, I am the only grandchild present. I am grateful for this, to have this time with her, alone. My mother is at the house too, as are my aunts, my father, my grandfather.

My grandfather sits alone in the kitchen. I cannot always gauge what he is thinking, his dementia washing over some of his emotions. I look at him, hold his hands. I tell him: *Thank you for everything*. It is one of the last sentences I shared with my grandmother before she died, too. It is the only thing I know how to say amidst loss.

My grandfather presses, asks what I mean (Dede, of course,

understood). I tell him: *Thank you for loving her.* That's enough.

I am amazed by Dede's beauty, even in death. I touch her face. She is no longer here, and yet she is, tangibly, under my thumb. Who decides what it means to be here? Are we not all always here, in some form?

My mother and one aunt join me in the bedroom. I pull up a prayer on my phone, read it aloud. I do not know if I am reading it for myself or for my grandmother or for her daughters. I only know that reading it, in this moment, is right.

I stay with Dede's body until I am ready to go. Just like a rose in a vase, I know that once her life force has been cut, all that which makes Dede herself will soon fade. I accept this, appreciate this—the beauty of a life well lived, now concluded.

I leave Dede, and I cry. My father is there to hold me. He does not say anything. I do not want him to. A parent's job is not always to know and to say. Sometimes it is simply to hold and to love.

Fear of death is unnecessary. We are afraid of dying because we are afraid of being alive, and to die is to have lived life to its completion, in its circle.

Show me the tears shed for a gerbera daisy. Show me the fear of cutting a collection of ageratums in order to bring their purple splendor inside.

We understand with cut flowers that beauty starts at the point of death, the space where life is removed. Death provides the beauty, is what makes it feasible.

Why then can't human death be the same? Just as a cut flower provides beauty, joy, after it has died, I believe that the deaths of those people we love can provide similar beauty.

Perhaps the deaths in my family are nothing more than new flowers for the vase. I see this in the images of Dede that now adorn our walls, in the way her beauty continues to fill our home in her photos, in her stories, in the mannerisms and expressions that her descendants all carry.

Her death, the death of all those we love, has filled our home with new beauty, new blooms. When the immediacy of their blooms has faded, I can press those petals, retain the memories of these people for the rest of my life.

I am afraid of death myself, I will not lie. I have questions, curiosity, concern. I know, though, that I am on a path to dying with peace—because I am on a path to living with peace. I believe that the more I return to nature, the more I understand my oneness with the world, the easier and simpler it will be to let go when my time has come.

All I am really trying to say is: there are not as many endings as we think.

Evergreens

Though it happens every year, I am always caught by surprise. Time. Spring turns to summer turns to fall turns to winter. The trees are bare and the animals are tucked away, and I don long overalls to work now, instead of the short versions I sport daily in seasons prior.

I have waited for this breathlessly at work since June, waited to witness the shift from flowers to evergreens—to see the Christmas decorations and stalwart plants in all their glory. It is a large piece of why I am still here. Here in Connecticut, in America, at this job. I want to absorb as much about plants as I possibly can before I return to Italy, and I know that seeing what the different seasons bring, which plants thrive in the cold, is an integral part of my education.

The greens take longer than normal to arrive from our growers. This year has been unusually warm up north, and the trees cannot be cut until they have experienced several frosts. If the weather has not chilled and the sap continues to flow in the plants when they are cut, they will dry out almost immediately. We must wait until the plants have gone dormant to take them down, must catch them sleeping, by surprise.

In May, when I began working at the nursery, I felt like a baby. Though I love plants, I lacked any formal knowledge of them besides what I had gleaned in random bouts of internet research. Despite this, I was thrust into the job, hands on and with immediacy, and I forced myself to learn. And learn, I did. I asked questions, of my bosses, of my coworkers. I read every book I could get my hands on. I quizzed myself to see if I could identify plants by only their flowers, then only their leaves. I learned about watering, soil conditions, lighting, hardiness. I filled myself up with plants, and the stories they tell. By summer's end I knew there was still much to learn, but I had given myself an incredible base of knowledge, and now felt confident answering customers' questions, guiding them in their plant selections dependent on their various needs.

When the greens finally arrive, this confidence crumbles around me. I feel like a baby at work all over again. Suddenly, I know nothing. Suddenly, plants become a foreign language to me once more. I knew I would have to learn more when the winter wares arrived, but I did not understand how drastic the change would feel, how alarming and total. I did not understand that I would feel exactly as I did when I first started, so lost and unintelligent and useless, so desperate to be helpful and yet endlessly mired in shame over how much I do not know. I want to admire the beauty of the greens, float through the fragrant balsam and tend to the shapes and textures of the cedar and pine and fir. I want to savor it, but I am overwhelmed, uncomfortably so.

The intensity of the novelty is compounded by the sudden rush of customers that flow in after Thanksgiving. People want holiday cheer, and who can blame them? They want it now. I find myself at a loss for words with our clients. After months at the nursery, I now have the knowledge to tell them anything they want to know about sages, petunias, begonias, fuchsias, anemones, cardinal vines, hydrangeas, heliotropes, mandevillas, marigolds, and more. I carry all this knowledge within me, hard-fought and fulfilling, and it is now useless, all these plants long dead or dormant. I do not know what to say.

I remind myself: This is why you are here. To learn. This is what you wanted. To learn something new requires starting over, knowing nothing. This is where beginnings happen. This is where the beauty lies.

I take a breath, dive in, and I learn. I learn that we have wreaths made of balsam, boxwood, fir, mixed greens, and magnolia. Magnolia wreaths instantly become my favorite, the leathery-looking leaves arranged in a flowing circle, almost too breathtaking to believe.

I learn about the different kinds of live plants out for sale, the evergreens large and small that will keep their color during the winter. I learn about Alberta spruces, andromeda, boxwood, osmanthus, juniper, and cypress. I study their textures and tones. I am caressed by their capacity to retain their color all winter when everything else has dropped their leaves. These remain.

I learn that all evergreens need water during the winter. Fresh cut greens, used for wreaths, garlands, and loose bunches that can be placed in planters, last longer when they receive rainfall or occasional misting. Live trees and shrubs, despite the dormancy they enter in wintertime, still need monthly waterings, or more if the weather is unseasonably warm. Their leaves continue to lose moisture, and we must replenish them, even when they are not actively growing.

I learn about perfectionism. One of my tasks at work during this period is taking loose branches of cedar and white pine and bunching them in clusters for sale. I become obsessive in my task, needing to find only the most perfect branches, desperate to create identical clusters. One of my coworkers shares with me the adage (a quote from Voltaire): *Perfect is the enemy of good.* Sometimes you have to just do, and make, and things just are as they are.

Another coworker sees me fretting with the bunches and tells me: *Don't stress. They do not have to be perfect; they just have to look full.* She tells me that most customers are not looking at every branch they pick up. They are just grabbing a bundle and throwing it in their wagon.

I take in what she is saying and understand it as true. It is not a slight at our customers, simply an acknowledgment of the reality. I am examining every branch and every twig with a scrutiny too intense, too dramatic for what the desired result requires. People just want to buy beautiful greens, plants, and pieces that make them feel cozy and festive. They are grabbing bunches of beauty where they see it, without the surgeon's eye that I have decided to apply.

I breathe this in, and I let go, beginning to collect branches with more abandon, less fear. Lo and behold, these new bunches are just as full, just as promising as the ones I languished over. Bundling up winter into a pretty package is simpler, more straightforward than it seems.

I learn that despite my rocky and terrified start with them, I love evergreens. I love them just as much, if not more, than all the flowering plants of summertime. I love them because they are still here, with me, still holding me during this time of rest when most of nature has faded away.

I notice for the first time that our yard at home is full of evergreens. It always has been, but I have taken this for granted, being constantly enclosed in a wall of color. In one corner by our garage stand tall and luscious arborvitaes. Beside them, several cedars. Next to these, two pine trees stand cock-eyed and courageous, a blanket of fallen orange needles at their feet. On the other side of our yard, countless cedars stand in a cluster, forming a barrier of green across two edges. I am warmed in the enclave of their breadth.

In the front and back yards alike, there are boxwoods of varying sizes, and by the front door a huge andromeda stands steady. Ivy covers most beds of mulch, and a small azalea bush lives next to the lawn. I am amazed that it has taken me so long to notice the presence of all these evergreens, the phenomena they produce. It has taken me twenty-five years to notice that while the rest of our neighborhood loses its color, our home is surrounded still, constantly, by green.

I become curious about the specific varieties of the cedar trees in our yard. It becomes a running joke between my parents and I; I ask them for the varietal name, and they, with large smiles plastered on their faces reply: *They're evergreens!* As though this answers me. I suppose, in a way, it does.

As someone obsessed with categorizing, growing, and monitoring plants, I cannot imagine planting such huge and expensive trees in my yard without knowing exactly which variety they are, exactly where they are native to, what they need, and anything else I can discover. I realize that though this is how I operate, how I will build a garden of my own one day, my parents have a different approach—and one that has worked out for them quite nicely, thank you very much.

My parents do not fret about exactly which trees they have placed around their home. All they care about is creating a lasting beauty for their family, which is, ultimately, everything. They have succeeded. I am reminded that knowledge is not a precursor to love, to creation. I am reminded that all it takes to surround a home with beauty, in any form, is the desire to do so. Evergreens, their ubiquity and presence, put everything in perspective.

I would be remiss to talk about evergreens without spending time on my favorite of them all: the rhododendron. I have hesitated to expound upon my love of her thus far, this elegant, ethereal being whom I care for so deeply. I hesitate because I fear I cannot do my love justice, fear I will not be able to represent the importance of this plant in the way I wish. I am still fearful, but I will try, regardless.

This summer, a month or so into my tenure at the garden center, my parents come in to shop. They have been coming to the nursery for years—it is how the owners know me well enough to feel secure in offering someone so inexperienced a job. It is always cause for small celebration when my parents stop in to poke around. I can spend time helping them, still technically doing my job, without the pressures I would normally feel with an unknown customer.

On this particular day my mother is seeking out plants to flank one of our doors. The hallway door that connects our garage to the house is tucked to the side, but it is the one we use to actually enter the house, and she wants something colorful to fill the space. She settles on two baby rhododendrons, perfectly spherical and fluffy. By the time I get home from work in the evening, my father has already gotten them into the ground, surrounded their crowns with mulch. It is a good system they have in the garden: my mother selects the beauty, my father carries it through to fruition.

These rhododendrons do not bloom this season, instead spend their energy getting settled in the ground. Once they are rooted, however, they quickly develop their buds for the following year, as most rhododendrons do. Next year, now established, they will join the rest of the more seasoned rhododendrons in our yard in putting on the most spectacular show.

We have two other rhododendrons. One is a truly massive shrub that reaches up and above my sister's second-floor bedroom window. Hot pink and decidedly stunning in bloom. The second of the plants stands to the left of our front door, a more mid-sized but equally impressive beauty which blossoms into a slightly lighter pink.

We do not know what shade our new rhododendrons are, the tags marking them almost immediately discarded and forgotten. We must wait for them to reveal themselves. Must wait for their brief but brilliant blooms.

To try to describe a rhododendron in flower feels like trying to describe true love. I can tell you about the big balls of brightly colored blooms that cover the plant. I can tell you that it feels like magic to drive around town in June, to see the walls of pink that line every street. I can tell you they look like cotton candy, like little homes for fairies, like joy and summer and sunshine and magic personified. I can tell you all these things, and I know I will not come close to capturing what a rhododendron can make one feel. It is beyond words, beyond explanation.

All I can really do is implore you to plant one of your own. To let the beauty of these evergreen miracles flourish outside your home.

The fact that rhododendrons are evergreen tells me there is, in fact, a God. Or several. Someone out there, up there, is painting beauty with the most generous brush. It would be enough if rhododendrons simply bloomed and then died back in the winter. That would be enough. Instead, their stunning clusters of deep green leaves remain all year long. Their little buds sit perched all winter, waiting for the right moment to burst forth. Rhododendrons remind me miracles are always possible, always happening.

I feel touched by evergreens as a concept. They do not have to be here, and yet here they are. Holding me when all else feels groundless. Cocooning me in green. Evergreens feel like they exist just for me. The beauty is, everyone can feel this, know this. That they exist for us all.

I want to understand why evergreens stay green while all the other trees and shrubs lose their leaves. I search for answers, but I am left dissatisfied. Here is what I find: evergreens maintain their leaves in order to conserve energy that would be spent recreating new leaves the following year. These plants are able to do this (maintain, conserve) because they hold onto more water than others do, and can use these water stores to support themselves.

I am dissatisfied because this is a human answer, and it gives me nothing. Trying to explain the habits of a plant with the words I have, the language I have, does not suffice. How do we know—how do we really know—why some trees stay green? How can any of us say for certain why they hold on the way they do?

There is so much diversity in the plant world, so much mystery and beauty, so much we cannot fully comprehend. We craft explanations, we have science to guide us, we can build stories, but we can never get inside the plants' minds, never truly understand their intentions.

To ask why the evergreen stays green taps into a space beyond words, beyond knowing, a space with questions free from definitive answers. Why do humans love each other, despite it all, knowing what we know? Why do people go on living when it would be just as simple not to? Why am I still here when I never thought I would make it this far? Some questions I cannot answer with certainty. Regardless, I try.

Why does the rhododendron stay green? To remind me that cold begets beauty, too. Why am I still here on this Earth? To share these lessons with you.

Jade

I AM LEARNING to be honest. I am learning that the only way to be myself is to live truthfully. At the same time, I know that truth hurts, that it can cause pain, and pain is something I try to avoid—for myself, for those I love. I do not always know where this leaves me. I do not always know how I am supposed to live.

I was not going to write this essay. When I decided I wanted to write this book months ago, I plotted it out, created a general outline. I wrote down the plants that have shaped me. I sketched the picture, I knew the story I wanted to tell. I wrote. I was almost done writing. Everything was clear. Everything was simple. And then I met you.

Now, I have more to say.

The last thing I expect to do before I move back to Italy is fall in love. It is not a thought in my mind, not a remote possibility. So much of what draws me back to Italy is the idea of starting a family there, creating a life there. Tending to a garden that can last generations. I figure—save the romance for Italy. Save the love.

I operate this way the whole time I am home, never thinking about men here as a real option, knowing I will soon be gone. And then I meet you. And I can still hear the Gods laughing.

You will break my heart, and I will break yours, because what we have is finite by nature. We keep using that word, finite, and it is. There are bounds to our love. I want to go there, you have your life here. We understand this. And yet, we are in love, and we have decided to honor that, for this brief moment in time. A blink, in the grand scheme of things.

I am pretending that this is about a plant when it is entirely about you, about us. But let me pretend, for the sake of my theme. Let me tether you to a plant, for the sake of my soul.

Crassula ovata. Jade plant. I decide that this is the plant I will leave you with, gift to you, before I go. You began collecting plants in your home the day we met—this is how we met. You came into the nursery to buy some. I had heard about you before. You are good friends with one of my work friends, Lee, and she thought we might hit it off. Later, she will tell me that she set us up because you are unfailingly kind and because we are both strong conversationalists. Two truths that have us fated from the start.

Lee introduces us the day you come in. You are not what I expect, who I expect, not at all. You purchase a watermelon peperomia and a trailing ivy this first day. I tell Lee to give you my number. She does, and that night you call.

I do not mean to fall in love with you. We have a first date, and I tell you afterward this cannot be. I care for you, but this cannot be. I think some part of me then already knew what I know now. That I want you. That I love you. I tell you we cannot be because I am protecting myself from the inevitable. I tell you we cannot be because I am terrified to be hurt again. Terrified to love.

I tell you we cannot be, cannot be together, but that we can be friends. We try this. We go out as a group to a bar in your neighborhood. You drink something alcoholic, I have a ginger beer. We chat. I touch your bracelet, a band of lapis beads. It is this moment that we begin to fall. Have we always been falling?

I am not doing a good job of pretending this is about a plant. At least I am being honest still, in my pretending. To be fair, as I started writing, I had every intention to talk about jade. Had every intention for that to be the majority of what I wrote. But you keep slipping in, keep sliding to the forefront of every thought, and I cannot help myself.

Let me try to explain my original intentions. I want to leave you with a jade because I want you to have something that can live forever, even though what exists between us cannot. I want to give you something eternal. If I cannot have you for that long, if I cannot build a life with you, then let me gift green longevity as consolation. Each of my gifts to you has been selfish, and full of love.

You do not want me to give up on my dreams. One night on the phone I say: *I know you will not ask me to. Will not ask me to stay here, with you and for you. But please know that if you did—ask—I would.*

You tell me: *If I were a more selfish man, I would ask.*

I have never known a love like this. A selfless love. I am trying to feel deserving of the honor. I am trying to remember, to be reminded, that if you can gift this type of love to me, someone else will, too. I am trying not to let the whole of our relationship be about the standards it will set for future ones. And at the same time, I do not know what else to tether myself to.

We are finite.

You are not selfish, and you will not ask me to put my dreams on hold. This is why I want to.

Just now I pause my writing, reach for my phone. I am always hoping to hear from you. We have said our goodbyes already, and yet each time we say goodbye it never is. We are trying to curb the pain. Trying to make it easier.

I am getting ahead of myself, except that's what we've been doing here all along. Rushing to the end, knowing what's to come. I have never known a love like this. I have never known love.

To say I have never known love is perhaps unfair to myself and to the many people who do in fact love me. What I should really say is this: I have never known romantic love. Not really, not truthfully. Not like this. It is warm. It is simple. It is home.

One of the most important qualities I discover about you is your unrelenting honesty. There is one moment, however, where I see this break. I tell you as I show you a favorite music video of mine (*M3LL155X* by FKA Twigs) how indescribably important this particular work of art is to me. I tell you that if you do not enjoy it, we are not compatible, and I can never speak to you again. I am joking, but barely. You tell me, in that case, you will have to lie if you dislike it. *You are my biggest weakness*, you say.

I find great comfort in the idea of plants outliving people. It is why jades have a special place in my heart—lush-looking succulents that can live for many decades. Some have been known to live for a century or more. Jades are often passed down from generation to generation, shifting caretakers of these constant creatures.

At work one day I stumble upon the largest jade I have ever seen. I eat my lunch each day in the office of one of the greenhouses, one that is closed to the public where excess plants are stored. My lunch is brief, and I usually have just enough time to eat before I head back to work.

One day, however, I finish lunch early and decide to explore. I exit the office, meander into the greenhouse, and it is here where I find it. It does not seem real, except I reach out and touch it to be sure. The woody trunk is just as solid and certain against my hand as the ground is beneath my feet. It is real, it is here.

The jade plant sits on a bench in the greenhouse, and nearly touches the roof. It has a thick main trunk larger than I can wrap my hand around, with a multitude of equally large and woody branches. It is an oasis.

The jade plants in the main greenhouse are all much smaller, ranging from ones with just a couple of leaf sets to ones that are about a foot tall. These young jades are still mostly green and fleshy, have not yet developed the woody trunk of their more mature counterpart. These jades look like any other succulent— green, with thick leaves. The large jade is different. It is a tree. It is a miracle.

I take a picture of this mammoth to send to my friend Darcy, a fellow plant lover. I want someone else to marvel at it with me, to witness it—to make it more real. I have a hard time believing beautiful beings with my own eyes.

Later I ask my boss how old the plant is. Thirty years. I am in awe. The prospect, the notion of nurturing a single plant for decades excites me, but it also terrifies. There is tremendous responsibility in taking care of something lasting. There is tremendous honor in knowing when one is ill-equipped to commit.

The time before I leave for Italy continues to dwindle. We have two months, then one month, then weeks. Before I know it, I will be gone. I decide to do what I have done for the people I love so many times before: I will gift you a plant to show you how I feel.

I have a collection of jades at home. These plants are small, each with just a couple of leaves. They begin as a gift from another work friend, Deedee (yes, there is sweet joy in having a coworker share a name with my late grandmother, sweet joy in saying that beloved name each day once again). Deedee prunes her eight-year-old plant in the summer, and when I mention that I have been interested in procuring a jade, she brings me a plastic bag of cuttings unprompted.

I take these cuttings home with me, possibility in my pocket. Some are fleshy and green, with a couple of leaf sets each. On others I can see wooden branches, some with little roots already started. I select five to plant, each unique, each at a different stage of progress. I cut the pieces that I want and lay them out to dry for a day. This allows the cuts I've made, the wounds on the plants, to callous over and heal. This way when I plant them, they will be less susceptible to rot. Protected.

After the cuttings are calloused, I plant them in matching terra cotta pots and set them on the windowsill. The waiting process begins. There are no signs of growth for the first month, as the plants begin to root into the soil. I check the progress of their rooting by occasionally giving a slight tug on their leaves. Once there is tension, resistance, I know the jades have settled in, rooted out.

After some time, the first signs of above-ground growth appear. One of the jades, a misshapen cutting with only one oblong leaf, is the first to begin. A minuscule leaf set appears one day, adjacent to the sole large leaf. These new leaves are so small that at first I am not certain what they are, if they could possibly be that which I do not dare hope for. I snap a picture of this baby growth, wanting proof and a point of comparison for later.

I am a big proponent of photographing plants, capturing their progress. I want to be able to look back on where they started, to see how far they have come. I do the same thing with myself, with my writing. I capture myself in a moment, mentally, so that one day I may look back and see: there is growth here. I have changed. It is harder to witness progress in real time, particularly when it is slow.

Jades are slow growers, like most succulents. They take their time. It takes a month for that first bit of new growth to resemble a leaf set, and even still it is minuscule. It will be at least several more months before those leaves reach full size, a couple inches long. It is easy to be patient with these lush creatures. They are so gorgeous, so full of water and life and love. They take their time, grow with care, develop with precision. Who would want to rush that?

The jades juxtapose our love. Whereas they take years to develop, our feelings for each other appear instantaneously. I keep telling you I want to freeze, to pause the moment, to live in this space with you for an eternity, for a second. One and the same. When I tell you this, I picture the jades. I picture their little leaves, expanding more gradually than anything I have ever witnessed. I want to crawl inside the leaves with you. I want to live in there, in that space where everything is slowed down, where we might have a chance to breathe. To be.

My sweet little jades sit still on my windowsill. They came from Deedee, whose plant came from a cutting of her aunt's plant eight years ago. Jades can be passed down and down and down, on and on and on. In giving, more are gained. In gifting jade, the legacy lives. I have such gratitude for Deedee, for gifting me these babies, for saving her cuttings and passing them along. I have such gratitude for them, for existing at all.

The other Dede, my grandmother, was a lover of jade, too. This love makes perfect sense to me. Jades are regal looking, majestic, so beautiful to gaze upon. Dede was a lover of beautiful things. She was a lover of life, and to hold a jade in one's hand feels a bit like holding all of the Earth, all of nature, in a single breath.

Dede kept a jade plant for decades. She divided it, pruned it, created new plants with it. My aunt has two plants from her, the only remaining ones now that Dede has passed. These jades live in my aunt's home, and will last for decades more with proper care. Them living still, despite their original caretaker having died, is a testament to their staying power, their ease of existence. Jades can live beyond death. I am hopeful that they can live beyond love, too.

I gift you a jade plant at an Italian restaurant, my favorite one in town. We go despite you not liking Italian food—I am aghast when I discover this, and joke that this is why you've decided not to follow me to Italy. Too many tomatoes.

I write a note which I place in the bag with the jade. In it, I tell you that jades like bright light, and that they want to get totally dry in between waterings. Later that night, I send you a video of a woman explaining proper watering techniques for the plant. I implore you to watch, to let her show you exactly how to treat it. I know you will be successful, know you can care for the jade, know you do not need all my prodding and suggestions. It's just that I am desperate for you to keep some part of me alive, with you.

I also tell you in my note that the jade I am gifting you is my favorite of the collection. It is my favorite because it was the least promising when it began, and has now put out more growth than all the rest. I was amazed at this for weeks until I realize that this plant, tucked into the right corner of a southwest-facing window, receives more sunlight than any of the other jades I have. It has grown so much because I have placed it somewhere where it can grow. A simple reminder that luck is just the universe making choices. I pray that we are making the right one.

I tell you in my note that I debated which jade to give you, and I did. I thought it over for weeks, looking at each, comparing and deliberating. No plant felt good enough, when what I wanted to give you was myself—my presence, my personhood. In the end, I had to choose a jade. In the end, the choice was simple. I gave the one I love most to the person who has taught me what it is to love at all.

You promise me that you will take care of the jade and I believe you. You promise me that you will always be a part of my life, that we will always be friends. I am trying hard to believe that too.

On a different day, I gift you my favorite book: *Bluets* by Maggie Nelson. It is, for me, a sad book. When friends who I recommend it to ask me to describe it, I tell them it is a book that honors sadness, honors the importance of the emotion, without glorifying it. I say this for years because I am ashamed of my own sadness, ashamed of its depths, and the glorification of an emotion of which I am ashamed feels wrong. I must provide the caveat, that this is not what Maggie Nelson is doing (glorifying), that she is simply holding us in the sadness, witnessing it.

I can admit now that there is glory in it. In the sadness. I am sad, deeply so, to lose you. Of this, I have no shame.

It is the moment I touch your lapis bracelet, the most gorgeous blue, that we both begin to fall. It feels appropriate to gift you a book about love and loss and blue beauty. An end to match the beginning. Endings are a funny thing. I know exactly how *Bluets* will end, exactly the feeling it will evoke, the exact arrangement of the final page and the way the words will hit my chest. I know exactly how it will end, and yet it still catches me every time, even before I have arrived there.

This is how I feel saying goodbye to you. I know it must be done, can sense the ache from the doorway, and yet even if it has already happened, it still must happen, for we cannot grieve that which we have not yet lost. We can try, but it will always be a facsimile. We must read through till the end, even and especially when we have read the book before. We must see it through. And yet still I tell you: I do not want to say goodbye. *Sogni d'oro*, I say instead. Sweet dreams.

Sogni d'oro is how one says sweet dreams in Italian, but it is not a precise translation. It literally means: dreams of gold. This is what I wish for you, waking and asleep. Dreams of gold. Beautiful blues and golden hues and a life full of all the color you deserve. May the greens hold you close when I cannot.

You have reminded me how beautiful I am, and for that I will be eternally grateful. You saw all of me and you said: I love it all. I look in the mirror now, and I love it all too.

I am older and wiser than I once was. I understand now, so importantly, that absolutely nothing lasts forever. But I also understand that if I allow myself to be wholly present, in each moment, then everything is always happening. Everything is always alive and here and now. You, because of how safe you make me feel, allow me to be present. Whole and here, in your arms. I can always access it then, the memory of us, because I was here for it. Because of you.

You are worth it all. You are worth the bittersweet taste in my mouth. You are worth the ache in my heart. You are worth this new kind of sorrow, one which I have not yet known. You are worth it.

I would not trade our moment for a lifetime, nor would I trade you for anyone in the world. You, exactly as you are, have been exactly what I need. All I ask, all I hope, is that you remember: I am as beautiful as you. You are as beautiful as me. Whatever exists in the space between us, don't forget that we are free.

The last man I was with, I did not tell my parents about. I did, however, tell Dede. She was the epitome of judgment-free, at least when it came to me, her beloved grandchild, and so I knew that anything, anyone, that makes me happy would put a smile on her face too.

Sitting out on her porch one day drinking chai lattes, she saw a look on my face. Love. I explained—yes, I have fallen into it. Because it is her, because I am me, I shared. I told her everything, and she was delighted. I did not know then that that love was not love. At least not when it stands in comparison to what I feel for you.

I do not tell my parents about you, either. Were Dede still here, know that I would race to tell her about you too.

The things we love shape the way we see the world. The different languages I speak help me to think in different colors. In Italian, I am more poetic, calmer in my body. Can see the world through a more fluid lens. Books and songs and other art have the same effect. When I read *Bluets*, when I watch an FKA Twigs music video, the world is tinged with sadness, a sadness surpassed only by the immense beauty these works also evoke. In these moments I see the world as it is: tragic, and unfathomably gorgeous. Is this my story too?

I picture the jade plant I gifted you. I can say with a relative degree of certainty that it lives in your bedroom, though I have yet to confirm this with you. I know your bedroom is the brightest room in your house, with windows lining two walls. I know you will have taken my instructions seriously, will want to give the plant a fighting chance. So I imagine the jade in your bedroom: properly lit and so close to your body as you sleep. The latter imagining is wish-fulfillment: let the jade take the space that I cannot.

Because jades grow so slowly, I am amazed by any and all growth they do put forth. Any small new leaf is a miracle. I learn that you think like a jade, that you know how to exist on their plane. *This is bliss*, you tell me, talking about us. You can appreciate a moment. I am jealous of you, that you are full of joy for what we have while I choke back tears. I ask you to teach me, and you do. You explain, you show. The jade is nothing more than a return of all you have given me. Peace in plant form.

I think of your jade plant and a part of me wonders if it is cruel to try to keep you tethered to me (me to you) with words and books and plants. I wonder if it is cruel to say I need to let go and yet am so unwilling to do that very thing.

I think cruelty requires intention, however, and I know

everything I have given, including these words here, has been given with love, with a love purer than I have ever known. I know I can trust that where love guides me, all I must do is follow.

You tell me one day: *You are so loveable, so easy to love.* You tell me: *That is your superpower.*

I believe you. You make me believe in my own goodness. You make me believe in the power of love, in my own capacity to love and be loved. Which is, in fact, the whole point of this whole thing. This brief and beautiful moment in time that we have shared.

I want more from you. I want to be with you always. You see it differently. You understand that we must live our separate lives, but that we are never far, never truly apart. You tell me: *Wherever you are, there I am.*

I need to believe you. Love is letting go. I am struggling to relinquish.

I am saddest when we are saying goodbye, and just after. I know the healing begins in this space. I keep reopening the wound. I am ready to suture it now.

I have been alone for so long. I never knew how beautiful it could feel to have a partner like this, a soulmate, someone to walk through this strange and gorgeous life with. I felt it, that beauty, that hand to hold, for but a moment. Now, I am alone again. I am afraid. And still I know, this is not enough reason to stay.

You are the end of this chapter in my life, and I know that, but I cannot see it yet, not fully. I cannot yet put perspective on something that I still hope, despite myself, will last forever. I play it forward, know it cannot. Know that if I stay for you, I will come to resent you. I know this is the end of this chapter, that you are the capstone to my time at home. I know. I can glimpse it. In time, I will feel it. In time, I will thank you.

Let me try now. Thank you for not asking me to stay. Thank you for not allowing me to. Thank you for loving me so selflessly, so fully, as I have never been loved before.

We try to say goodbye so many times over. We say goodbye

on the phone, in person, via text. I say goodbye more. You have made your peace already, have found a wave to ride in the ocean of uncertainty. I am less stable, less mature, less prepared. I am afraid. I try to say goodbye before the real goodbye because I have never had so much to fear, so much to lose. I have never known the fear of one's heart splitting in two, torn between a place and a person. The goodbyes do nothing to assuage this.

I send a message to a friend recently, one that I do not want to write, because to write it is to acknowledge reality. I tell her: *I'm so afraid to go back to Italy and leave him. I'm afraid because he is so good to me, and I'm afraid I will never find that again. What I'm realizing though is there is beauty in the fear. All my growth has happened when I dove into new challenges, new phases of my life, full of fear. This, leaving him, is an opportunity for growth. It's terrifying, and that's beautiful. This is opening a space for me to transform.*

I know this in my bones, that going back to Italy is right. Leaving this man whom I love is the right thing. So why does it feel so unnatural? Why do I feel like an overwatered jade, drowning and helpless?

Know that when I look back on this moment in time that we have shared, I will view it only with love. *Forgive me*, I tell you. *I am trying to imagine a life that could be better than one with you. Forgive me as my imagination catches up to the reality of your beauty.* Know that every second of my time with you, even the sadness, was spurred by a love greater than I have ever known. A love that is home.

You are a love worth all the loss. You are a love I can never lose. *You were prolific*, you tell me. You tell me you are not creative, and yet the words you choose to share with me are Degas' dancers on my heart. You spin beauty out of thin air, weave it between my ribs.

I want to call you, want to delete all these words off the page and speak them to you instead. I want to run over to your house and come inside and never leave, just burrow into your chest and make a home there. Find a home in you.

I know that I can if I so choose. I can choose you. Can choose this love. The option is on the table. No one is forcing me to leave.

Except. Except you have loved me in such a way that I refuse to forsake myself. Not for you, not for anyone. To love you properly, I must first love myself. And to love myself, I must go.

When I realize this, that I must go to Italy still, that I must leave you, I weep. It is the kind of crying I partake in after someone dies, a kind of crying I have not witnessed in myself in many months. And suddenly I see. I cry for you like I cried for my grandma and my grandpa and my friends and my dog and all the losses I have ever known. I have wept and sobbed for each. And I see: this is love. This is what a life full of love is. It is a life full of equal and tremendous loss. And I see: I could not change that even if I tried. And I see: I would not change it even if I could.

When I arrive in Rome, my first plant purchase will be a jade. I will keep it on the windowsill and will think of you as I care for it. I will think of me, too. I will think about my growth and all it has allowed for. I will think of all the love that is possible in my life if I just keep growing, bit by bit.

I know we are never far from each other because of the common languages we now share. Languages I already spoke, that you learned, because you love me enough to want to understand each part of me. Thank you for learning how I speak. Thank you for making even distance unspeakably sweet.

I am done pretending this is about a plant now. Know that this is your legacy in me: unrelenting honesty. Plus all the laughter. Plus all the love.

Every word in this piece is for you, not the plants. Know that I love jade like I love breathing. Know that I love you even more.

Compost

Everything is Earth.

Everything that exists on this planet is part of it, comes from it. Every part of my body is composed of the same carbon, the same nutrients and molecules that are shared with every plant, every animal, every living entity. We are all coming from the same source. All stemming from the same life. We are all from the same soil.

In the fall I watch as the leaves change colors. As a child, I hated raking (too much work, too much focus), but I would love to watch my father rake, the subsequent pile of leaves that appeared becoming my playpen. I jumped into the piles, feeling the heady Earth crunch under my weight. The smell was intoxicating, the feeling delicious beyond belief. I would climb inside the giant leaf bags, hidden from the world in total darkness. There was something so serene in being a child in a leaf bag, surrounded by the crisp fall scents. Utter safety, utter joy.

As a child, I did not understand that the colorful leaves that fall from the trees are simply dead. That the reason they have fallen is because they are no longer producing energy, have died, have been let go. Understanding this as an adult brings heartbreak and wonder. You understand—there is beauty in death. There is love in letting go.

How are the trees able to let go with such ease when the weather changes? They are a part of nature, and they understand their place. They understand, they feel, that to let go is not to lose. They understand, they feel, that everything remains. Everything is always right here.

Every year after my father rakes all the leaves, he shuffles the big bags off to the dump. He's done this my whole life, and yet it never occurred to me to tag along, to see the composting site there for myself. One day I finally ask to join him.

My father is excited, blatantly, to bring me on this adventure. He has already piled the bags into the car. It's a quick drive from our house to the dump. We drive past the sites for regular waste and head back to the composting section. I am stunned by what I see, what a gem has been hidden in plain sight this whole time.

I see walls of compost. Mountains of it higher than I can process. Toward the bottom, compostable bags full of lawn clippings and leaves pool in masses. Further up the pile, gorgeous brown compost is all the eye can see. It looks lush, warm, inviting. It looks like home.

There is such beauty in a compost pile, because death is the most giving thing on Earth. Don't believe me? Stick your hand in the middle of a warm pile of compost. Feel death in your hands. Play with it, work it through your fingers, and tell me it isn't the most generative thing you've ever held. Compost is full of death and life, simultaneously. It is the meeting place between these seemingly disparate worlds.

I become enamored with our compost pile at work. It is a huge mound that lives out back behind the greenhouses next to a small pond on the property, one which dries out and fills as the weather changes. We have compost bins scattered everywhere, into which we place any spent bits of plant or soil. At the end of each day, one of the tasks is collecting the compost from all the bins and depositing it onto the compost pile. I rush excitedly toward the bins, eager for this duty.

I am taught with the compost pile to dump on top, not on the side. The reason for this soon becomes clear, as each day the pile grows exponentially, and the only way to slow the spread is to try to get as much of the compost on top of the heap as possible, rather than letting it extend further out.

Returning to the compost daily allows me to see just how quickly it morphs, how alive it is. Each day, new plants are added—sometimes just bits of leaves and clippings, other days whole huge plants which have rotted or naturally faded out of season. Every piece of Earth we have is returned to this one pile.

We have a lot of euphemisms for composting at work, because we do not want the customers to know when we are getting rid of plants. Too many images of waste without an understanding of where it all goes. Instead, Bonnie, my boss, will ask me to take plants "for a walk"—their final walk, back to the ground.

Bonnie tells me there is catharsis in composting, and I believe her. One day, she has me compost a huge array of vegetables which have been overtaken by mildew. There is no saving these plants from the fungus now, and so it is time to let them go.

Many of these vegetables are in six-packs, planted as plugs—a plastic pot only about 1-inch across and 2-inches deep, just large enough for seedlings to get started in before they are planted in a larger pot or the ground. Composting plants that are in six-packs is a more involved process than I first understand. It requires a lot of removal. Removing each individual plug from the pack. Removing any and all tags. It is tedious, and I love every moment of it.

I place all the bits into a wheelbarrow (large composting projects fill up an individual compost bin too quickly for them to be efficient to use), and I wheel the whole thing over to the pile. The catharsis begins. I start grabbing vegetables by their leaves and stems, hurling and chucking them atop the pile.

I cannot help but laugh, a childlike laughter that rumbles from my belly. I feel so alive. I am twenty-five years old, and I have never felt younger or freer than in this moment, dancing in the dirt and swinging zucchinis and squash atop a mound of plants. Oh, what joy there is in nature. Oh, what pure, accessible joy.

I want to dive into the compost pile. I want to be subsumed by it. I admire the plants, the way they make it their home. Many of the plants start to break down and decompose soon after they are thrown into the pile. They join in, allow themselves to be consumed by the bacteria and fungi, allow themselves to return to the warm humus in the center.

Other plants, however, take a different approach. Some of these, rather than sinking into the pile, are bolstered by it. They utilize the rich nutrients the decaying matter provides, and instead of doing the same (decay), they grow. This is how we come to end up with a wide field of pink phlox spreading across the top of the pile. This is how a cluster of impatiens, tossed to the side of the pile after they are devoured by deer, survives, then thrives. There is a continuous circle of life and death in compost.

One day while chatting with my dear friend Darcy, we get into a discussion on death. Both of us readily admit to our fears surrounding death, and our fascination with it—the process of it. Darcy, unprompted, tells me: *When I die, just throw my body in the woods.* I laugh at this, tell her I will be happy to oblige. I note that it may be awkward, if I outlive her, to courteously inform her family that she is to be stripped naked and laid in the dirt somewhere. I say I will do it regardless. It is moments like these that I am reminded why I choose the friends I do. A joke that's not a joke, one that shows me she understands.

As humans we have such formality around death, and such different approaches. Every culture has rituals, every family their own means of coping, remembering, grieving. I grew up in a home where death was not discussed, the emotions of it never acknowledged. I remember the first death I encountered, my great-grandmother's. The tremendous gravity of it.

I remember being tucked away in the corner of my bedroom in a little reading nook filled with floor pillows. I remember my father coming into my room, telling me great-grandma had passed away. I remember not grasping that, not at all. When is she coming back? When is she coming back?

I can see now that she has been here all along.

I want to dive into the compost pile, I want to live in there. Not because I am ready to die yet. I hope I have a long full life ahead of me, one that will bring me a wrinkled face and bountiful creation.

I want to live in the compost pile because it is my original home. Every piece of my body was formed by the energy that came from the ground. Each plant that fed each animal that fed and formed my body—every molecule in me found its start in some piece of the Earth. I want to live in the compost pile because it is me. We are the same stuff. It's another body, and a warm one, and I want to get cozy in it.

There has always been a heaviness around death in my family, a weight to it. I think it is because we do not talk about it. We do not let it breathe. We have to let the death out. At work we use the tractor to turn the compost pile. Death needs air to break down, needs movement. We have to play with death a bit, to get the life out of it.

I have abandoned my family's understanding of death, have shaped my own, one that holds me. I do not consider myself religious, have no God. What I believe in is nature. I believe nature is a power greater than us all. I believe all of us have our unique and necessary place in nature, one we may not fully grasp but that is held for us regardless. I believe that nature is not something we ever leave. We are all Nature, all a part of her dance, forever. The beauty of our bodies morphing into the beauty of flowers shifting into the beauty of butterflies. Nature is continuously transforming herself; we are intrinsically a part of this transformation.

I take this understanding, these beliefs, and I say: death can be easy. Death can be light. Death can be fun and beautiful and gorgeous, when we understand it not as something tragic, but rather as the most tremendously important piece of our little dance called Nature. Death can be as simple as hurling a rotten cabbage on top of the compost pile and watching it land, laughing as it falls.

I come to understand the compost pile as a hopeful microcosm of the Earth as a whole. What I see in the compost in real time, the ebb and flow and reciprocity between all life and death, I apply to my understanding of the planet at large. We are all constantly coming from and returning to the Earth. Every single thing, even the computer in my lap and the dust in the air, every entity we interact with all has the same home. This Earth. This Universe. This gorgeous circular moment called Nature. We are always here.

I watch a documentary recently, one that further alters how I see the world. It is called *Fantastic Fungi* (2019) and it is about exactly that. While fungi are not plants, exist in the tree of life in a kingdom all their own, their relationship with plants is fascinating and, appropriately, fantastic.

I learn from this documentary that fungi "are the digestive tracts of" nature, that they play an essential role in the decomposition process. It seems so obvious once it is explained to me, but I did not see that before, the necessity of these decomposers.

Mold makes us squeamish because it signals death. But without mold, without the fungi who break down organic matter, nothing would be able to return to the soil, become soil. I find myself emotional watching this film, overwhelmed by the relationships that exist in nature. Fungi feed on us all, and then feed us all. We are all feeding and healing each other, being fed and healed, reaching out across kingdoms of life with a single truth: we are all from here—we are all one.

I am no different than the smallest bacteria cell, no different than the tallest sequoia. Every blade of grass is equal to every mushroom is equal to every worm swirling through the dirt. For we are all one thing: Nature. We are Nature in a constant state of transfiguration. We, as one, are whole.

I love watching things break down. Love to watch the pieces of the puzzle fall into place. Decomposition is a simplification. Demystification. Taking a multitude of difference and breaking it down until I can see: this is all the same. This is all the same.

Every piece making up the same grand picture, one incomplete without the whole.

When I was little one of my favorite activities was sitting outside and placing some food item on the ground. I would do this when I would see an ant or two, knowing that if one of them found food, they would go tell all their little ant friends and they would all come feast. I found great magic in placing that chip or whatever I was nibbling on, and watching the ants, one by one, march over and grab their share. After some time, what was once there had disappeared, transformed into energy for the ants.

We can look at life as hunting and killing and suffering and death, or we can look at life as feeding each other, as leaving chips for ants and understanding that everything and everyone must die—and what a gorgeous notion that is. We all die, and this whole great world, this whole universe, these things which we are always a part of, live on.

When I grew up, I stopped leaving chips for ants. Instead, I now watch the breakdown of life with plants. At home in the garden, I pluck leaves here and there, dead ones. Instead of collecting all of them in a pile, I will save one or two to leave on a bed of mulch. I'll watch these for weeks, watch them break down. It is a slow process when they sit on their own like this, and I find deep satisfaction in seeing a leaf, bit by bit, slowly return to soil.

I tell my father this year not to clean up all the leaves. One of my coworkers teaches me how important dead leaves are, how important they are for nature, for insects and the soil. Of course. In nature, in forests, the floor is not bare. It is shrouded in leaves, in dead plant matter. This is how nature maintains itself—through the feedings of death. When we clear away all the leaves, all the dead plant matter, we also clear away the possibility for new life.

My father clears the leaves off the lawn, leaving his green grass pristine, but he allows for the leaves that pile up on the beds of mulch, and allows the dead daylilies and other perennials to remain too. Beauty in compromise, rejuvenated soil to benefit all.

Sometimes I get so scared, paralyzingly so, about the state of the Earth. I am afraid that we have already destroyed too much of her, ripped too much out of her, built too much up on top of her. I wonder, is she okay down there? And then I remember— everything is Earth. We may be reconfiguring her with a heavy human hand, but she can return to herself. We simply must allow her to do so.

I find comfort in looking at pictures of abandoned areas. Small-scale, like no longer used mall complexes, and large scale, like the city of Chernobyl. I am comforted by these images because I see what can happen when nature is allowed to run its course, to not be so controlled. I see the way life grows out of everything, every crevice in every building.

It is not that I think humans must abandon all Earth in order for nature to heal. The opposite, in fact. Humans must understand our place on Earth, our intrinsic connection to every piece of it. We are valuable here, we are necessary, we are a part of this, but we must listen. We must relinquish control and let nature regain it. This is the space where healing begins.

I look down my own street, see the paved road and feel an aching for the constrained ground underneath. It looks like it is strapped into too-tight clothing. I wonder if it can breathe. Then I glance further, see the edge of the road, see a chunk of the pavement cracking, warm wet Earth poking out through the crevice.

Earth is here. Underneath it all. In it all. Earth is always here. Can you feel her beneath your feet? Do you feel her in your own arms? Can you feel the water of every ocean coursing through you, the carbon and minerals of the ground in your blood?

Collectively, humans have become detached from the Earth. We are floating, separated, and we are aching. We are all aching. We deserve better.

All you have to do is dig a little and see: it is all Earth. There she is. There we are. Let us care for her. Let us tend to her. Let us plant seeds, let us compost, let us return to the Earth, every moment of every day. I promise, in healing her, we inevitably heal ourselves. I know this, am living proof. Tending to the green has given me so much more than I have given her. Nature is doling love out freely—we must only place our hands out, receive. Give thanks. Every one of us has our feet in the dirt.

I picture my body after I have breathed my last breath. It is an old body. My body is placed upon the compost, at long last. Bare. Alone, and completely held. Animals will consume my flesh. Insects and bacteria will feast. Fungi will work to break me down, decompose the remains. From where my body was, new life shall appear. I envision this, this transformation. Arms dissolving into flowers, toes into tree trunks. All the birds that will one day feed from the nectar of my body, my blood. All the butterflies and bees that will benefit. I only lament the fact that I will not be there to see it, to witness it.

I pause. Aren't I already seeing it, right now? There, right now? Here, right now? Witnessing the continuous flow of nature, of my body, of the pull and ebb and waves of the whole thing? The way we are all rocking and moving as one? The way we all came from the stars and the soil and the way we're all going back there, will live there together once more? Every piece of me is flower food. Every piece of me is the universe come alive. To return to the Earth is to return home.

I cannot lament the fact that I won't be there to see this return, won't be there to witness my body transform. I cannot lament this because I am there. Am here. I have been here, there, all along. I came from the Earth, I tend to the Earth, I will return to the Earth once more.

I am here. In this moment, I exist as this body. At some point, I will die, and this body will break down. What beauty in that, in the impermanence of it all, and in the continuance. This brief moment of consciousness, and the assured path home. Soon I will return to the home which I feel but cannot remember. Soon I will remember what it is like to be all life at once, part of the beating heart of the Earth. Soon I will be from the soil someday.

Buddleja

THIS IS the end and the beginning. Every other essay in this book I write out of order, and piecemeal, flitting back and forth between them, wherever my mind takes me. This piece I save. This comes after every other word is written, everything else has been said. This is the beginning and the end, which are one and the same.

It begins with death: my grandmother's. It feels only right that this whole thing should end there too. It is Dede's death that spurs not only this project, but all my growth this year. Without her passing, I would not be where I am. And so, I save this for last. The beginning. The end.

I consider myself tremendously lucky to have witnessed Dede's final week of life. She had the awareness, the presence, to understand her life cycle was nearing its end. She told us as much, and her family was able to spend those last days with her.

I have yet to write about this time, those final days, because I am scared that once I do, those memories will leave my body. I am afraid because I think I know they need to. I think I have been holding the beauty and the pain of her final week so tightly to my chest for over a year now. I think it is time to let it go. To leave it right here, on these pages.

To watch someone die is a gift, if that person is ready to go. Just before Dede makes her pronouncement (*I have a few days left*), I go to see her. I have been talking to her on the phone often, reading books to her over video calls now that it's hard for her to read herself, but I have not seen her in person in a while. I go in to visit, and she is asleep. Her body looks weak, frail. But when she opens her eyes, it is the same Dede I have always known. There is a vibrancy and spirit to her that inspires even the most ardent cynic.

We sit and chat about politics, and I tell her about my plans for Italy. It is a lovely visit. Two days later, I am standing in the bathroom when my father comes by to tell me and my sister: Dede is not well.

We all get in the car, race to her house, and it is then when she tells us, so calmly, so serenely: *I have a few days left.* There is such tranquility in this statement. She has surrendered to life, to nature, and she is at peace. It emanates from her. I seek to enfold myself in it.

Over the course of the next few days, we take turns sitting by her bedside. Sometimes we gather in groups, but mostly one on one, each wanting our precious final moments alone with the matriarch who has shaped us all. I bring over the book we are in the midst of, have been reading over the phone—*Severance*, by Ling Ma—and read her pages at a time. The book still sits on my shelf, unfinished—I have yet to pick it up since.

I also bring over several books of poetry, ones I have not yet read. I want to learn alongside my grandmother one last time. We sit and read and talk, and it is like every other time before, even though we know there will be no more times like it in the future. Why not enjoy it then, once more?

At one point I pull up on my phone my favorite poem of all time: "Wild Geese" by Mary Oliver. It is a poem handed down to me by my mother many years ago, one I turn to constantly. I read it to Dede once. She smiles, looks at me, and says: *Read it again.* And so I do. A poem handed from mother to daughter to grandmother. Everything is running in a circle, all the time.

On her final truly cogent day, I wear a shirt over to the house that she gifted me for Christmas a few years ago. It is silk, Italian, blue. Cropped at the waist with a low V-neck and billowing sleeves. It is so Dede, and so Eleanor, and so perfect to wear to her deathbed.

I have said a thousand times over that Dede's death perfectly suited her life. She lived a life full of beauty, full of poetry and good food and kind souls. So it is only fitting that when it is time for her to die, she does it in the same fashion. She is read to. We play music for her. My father drives a few towns over to buy her the most delicious fried chicken from a particular grocery store, at her request. When Dede asks my mother to spray a little perfume on her, my mother obliges, spritzing once on her pillow. Dede shakes her head. No, she silently chastises, and she leans her neck over, makes clear that she wants the gorgeous scent sprayed as close to her nose as possible. What she wants, she receives, and we are all grateful to fill her life with beauty once more.

The perfume my mother sprayed is the one Dede wore religiously. It is the one I wear right now as I write these words. Mimosa and Cardamom, from Jo Malone. After Dede passes, my mother buys bottles of the perfume for myself, my sister, my aunts, as well as for Dede's three caretakers. At first when I would spray it, it smelled like Dede to me. Now when I use it, it smells like me. I think that is the way it's supposed to go.

When I find myself becoming emotional at Dede's, I take a step outside. I go out back, to the garden, bedraggled but still green. Trees and grass surround me, hold me, long before I know that this is what they are doing. I think, what would Dede do in this moment, so full of sadness and anticipatory grief and simultaneously so full of love—absolutely bursting with gratitude for another human?

She would dance. I take out my phone, set it up to record on a tree stump a few feet away, and I dance. I let everything I'm feeling out of my body, feel the way the sleeves of the shirt billow against my skin in the movement. I twirl, and sway, lift my leg in a slow *développé*. I move.

After I am done, after the tears have dried, I return inside.

I show Dede the video of my dancing, a dance I do just for her, just for me, and she marvels. I am always searching for beauty in every moment, for myself and for those I love. She taught me this way of being.

I feel indescribable gratitude for the final words that are exchanged between Dede and me. I am able to say everything I need to say, and I receive enough from her to carry me through a lifetime.

I tell her: *Thank you for everything.* She tells me, *Thank you, too.* I tell her: *So much of the best of me comes from you,* and this makes her smile.

I tell her: *Thank you for helping me to believe, to believe in something greater than myself. You opened my eyes.* She is moved by this, this growth in me. When I was a child, a teen, Dede and I would get into heated intellectual debates about the afterlife. She, a devout Russian Orthodox Christian, would talk about individuals who have experienced the afterlife. People who had medically died and come back to life and had experienced something beautiful, otherworldly. She would posit this as proof that there is a God, that there is a life beyond death.

I would scoff at this, listing off possible scientific explanations for what these people might have experienced. A flood of endorphins at the time of death. Hallucinations in response to extreme trauma. I refused to accept that a spiritual answer was possible, refused to believe there is anything more, anything beyond.

Dede would simply smile. She loved debating with me, told me it made her feel like she was in college again. It was one of our favorite activities together: find a contentious topic, pick a side, battle it out. It made us both feel energized, alive, and respected.

Dede would simply smile. She did not feel offended that I disputed so intensely her understanding of the world, of spirituality and religion and afterlife. She believed. She felt no need to convince me either (beyond playful debate), and now I can see why. Dede believed in a truth so strongly, held her belief so purely, that she felt no need to convince anyone of it. It was hers, and that was enough.

As she begins to slip away, Dede tells one of her friends who comes to see her: *My head is in Jesus's lap now*. She believes it to be true, and so it is, and what beauty in that. I do not believe the same things as her, but I believe in her belief, and that is enough for me.

While she is dying, I walk into her room after a break and say, loudly: *HELLO BEAUTIFUL!* Her face lights up at this proclamation, she absolutely beams. It reminds me of a time when I was in middle school, and Dede met the mother of a friend of mine. This mother tells her, unprompted, how beautiful she is, and it practically moves Dede to tears. I think Dede and I are alike in this regard—both so blatantly beautiful, know it, and yet are so deeply moved by hearing it from others. It is not vanity, I decide. It is a deep appreciation for all the beauty of the world, and an immovable understanding that that beauty starts in oneself.

I do not like goodbyes. I do not like finality, permanence. I say goodbye to Dede multiple times, multiple instances on each day. I do not know which one will be last, and so I want to say it each time. *Goodbye. I love you.*

I spend time massaging Dede's feet. She is such a physical person, so in tune with her body, so much like me, and so I take out one of her many jars of lotion, remove her socks, and work my hands into her feet. They are bruised, unsightly, and so beautiful—because they are hers. I feel grateful to provide ease to her body in this moment. I feel frustrated that I cannot do more. I understand, too—maybe this is enough. Maybe this is all it needs to be.

At one point Dede asks me if I want to hug her, and I realize, oh yes, I do. I lean down, hug her, hold her, and I let the tears flow. I have been avoiding crying in front of her. Our whole family has. We do not want her to see our pain, see our loss. I decide: let her see. Let her see how much she means to me. Let her see all the love I feel. Let it flow.

The final words Dede says to me, that feel too perfect to be true: *Have a blessed life*. I have it now, Dede. It's here. Thanks to me. Thanks to you.

After one of my goodbyes, I step outside into the summer sun. I take a quick walk down the road, let my muscles stretch. I find a bush to plop down beside, and I weep. I let the tears pour out of me once more, held in my grief.

When I am done crying, I glance up and am greeted by the most beautiful vision. A cluster of white butterflies. There must be at least a dozen, dancing near me. The bush is all green, no flowers in sight for the butterflies to be seeking, yet here they are, fluttering about. I decide in this moment: this is the universe saying hello. This is a sign. This is Dede.

After her death, butterflies become my way of finding Dede in the world. It is a symbolism of choice, by design, and it is one I embrace. Symbols, the meaning we assign to them, are for ourselves. For Dede, Jesus was a sign of peace, of comfort. For me, I find comfort in the butterflies. Whatever holds us, whatever makes this thing called life beautiful and meaningful—there is value there.

While in Italy, after Dede's passing, I commend myself on choosing the symbol of butterflies to represent her. They are abundant. I find the real thing on every plant, I see them in art, on clothing, as a part of jewelry.

The streets of Florence are a museum unto themselves. It is a combination of the old and new—around one corner, an ancient fresco stands along a building wall. Loop around the next corner, and magnificent and recent graffiti art is sprayed across another. I find myself slowing down on the streets, desperate to see it all.

On one such exploration, I find a gorgeous graffiti-painted butterfly on a wall. I snap a picture, send it to my mother. I have told her already what butterflies mean to me, and she adopts the symbol for herself. We start sending butterflies back and forth to each other wherever we find them. Abundant beauty, to remember another.

In Venice, on the island of Giudecca where I live, I find myself walking even more than in Florence. Venice is the most walkable city I have ever been in, because it is the only option. You can travel by boat, or you can walk, and that is it. There are no cars, no bikes, only pedestrians and captains. I, unable to operate the family's boats, walk everywhere.

One day, after dropping off the girl I am nannying at her ballet lesson, I decide to take a long and more winding route home. Venice is full of random pathways, and I always feel like a little kid, exploring every nook and cranny. It reminds me of getting purposefully lost in the woods, knowing that something potentially magical is around every bend.

I am walking home, winding through the alleys and walkways of Giudecca, when I see it. A green wall, maybe twenty feet long and seven feet high. It is a dark green paint, and the wall stands on its own, not attached to any building I can see—perhaps walling in a garden or courtyard, though I can't be certain. I stand gobsmacked. Covering the whole wall is a mass of painted butterflies. Yellow, orange, purple, pink, and red-painted insects spread their wings along the expanse.

I stand in front of this wall for I don't know how long. I just stand and stare. Hello, Dede. Hello, gorgeous universe who is holding me always, smiling at me always. I stare at this wall, and I know in my core: I am so held. I am so loved.

When I begin my job at the garden center, I learn that certain plants are more attractive to pollinators than others. I become intrigued by which plants will draw in the butterflies best. I learn that butterflies, generally, are drawn to plants with tubular flowers and flower structures that have room for them to land on—these are the easiest for them to push their proboscis into, easiest to remain steady on while they feast. Daily I find butterflies swarming on plants like cuphea, with their long, elegant necks. I see them perched and clustered around plants like lantana, with their field of circular flowers that the pollinators can plop on with ease.

Lantanas become one of my favorite flowers—not only are

there butterflies constantly swarming over them, but I find the smell of them absolutely intoxicating. I learn that some people are in fact repulsed by the scent, but this does not deter me from my love. While lantanas are grown as annuals here, living only for a single summer, I learn that in much of Italy, lantanas are grown as perennial shrubs. This notion excites me, and I decide that when I return to Italy, when I start building my roots there, I will plant a small lantana bush. I will watch the butterflies enjoy it, and I will watch it grow.

I soon learn about another plant which is a butterfly magnet: buddleja. Buddleja is also known as the butterfly bush, and this nickname is certainly appropriate. No other plant that I witness attracts as many butterflies as the buddleja. They are drawn to it by a force greater than hunger, greater than a desire for sustenance. When I watch the butterflies on the buddleja, I am watching a love story.

Buddleja is a genus encompassing a multitude of perennial shrub species. These shrubs vary in color, size, and bloom time, yet all are equally magnificent at attracting butterflies to their petals. The buddleja flowers exist in a long, tube-like grouping, these tubes covering the entirety of the bush. Buddlejas come in white, blue, purple, pink, orange, violet, in a wide variety of shades of each. They are incredible bloomers, beginning to show color in early to mid-summer and lasting into September. There is great beauty in these vibrant blossoms, yet the real beauty, for me, comes in the life they attract. The butterflies they bring near.

We sell buddlejas at the garden center, mid-size ones. They stand tucked in one corner of the property, along with all the other shrubs we carry: hydrangeas, rhododendrons, lilacs, viburnum, holly, boxwood, beautyberry, and more. Our buddlejas for sale come in various shades of pinks and purples, with one random white tucked in. I love walking amongst them, feeling the way their long, feather-like plumes tickle my skin.

There are the buddlejas for sale and then there are two buddlejas which live on the property, have their roots in the grounds of the garden center. Both of the latter are several decades old. A white one stands wide and towering above me next to the parking lot. The other, a stunning pink, lives out back, leaning up against a raised bed.

One day, I am tasked with cleaning the white planted buddleja. It is mid-August, and while the shrub is still putting out blooms, it has many spent flowers as well—ones that have faded and died and now remain attached to the plant, a sad-looking brown. I am told to cut back all the spent flowers I can reach. I work my way around the base with my shears, snipping as I go.

This buddleja is huge, after twenty or so years of growth. Each year, the owner cuts the buddleja in half to encourage it to grow more from the base. Doing so has turned this once small and lanky shrub into what feels like a forest unto itself. A multitude of thick branches jut from the Earth, and the whole thing is huge and ever-growing. I am continuously amazed that all we have to do to create beauty in this world, life in this world, is place a plant in the ground. We place a plant in the ground and it grows. Is that not a miracle?

Once I have snipped all the flowers I can reach, I get up on a stone bench that sits next to the buddleja, and grasp for higher branches. I have always had a fear of heights, nothing pathological, but certainly a reasonable concern for my safety whenever I am off the ground. I am a Capricorn, an Earth sign, a nature lover, and I like my feet planted firmly on solid soil. So even now, in this moment, standing up on the bench, I can feel my heart race. I never want to fall.

I hold the thicker branches to keep myself steady, plucking away bits of dead flowers and dropping them in the compost bin on the ground. I know it is not a far drop, but I have fear, and I honor that fear. I feel my heart race a bit. I am so determined to make the bush look as beautiful as possible, but am so nervous for the drop. It is worth the risk.

I feel something brush up against my hand as I work. I glance down and see a small white butterfly floating by. Then, another.

I look around me and realize that there are dozens of butterflies all over the massive buddleja. I had been so consumed by my anxiety over slipping and falling that I do not notice the magic swirling around me until it is directly in my face, on my skin. I glance around, look at all the butterflies waving hello, and I feel my feet sink into the bench, which sinks into the ground. The universe, the Earth, is always holding me.

Symbols are the lens we see life through. We can decide that everything is meaningless, unconnected, or we can decide that everything is utterly entwined, that everything means something, signals something. The colors and shapes of life are the same either way—it is how we feel about them that is altered when we decide to see beauty in everything. We can look at a butterfly and say: this is just an insect flying by. I see a butterfly and choose to see my grandmother saying hello, reminding me that all life is one.

A couple weeks before my 21st birthday, a beautiful friend of mine, David, dies. It is unexpected, tragic, and it hurts more than anything I have ever known. Everyone who knows this man is deeply affected. David was one of those people who radiated beauty, warmth, love. To be around him was to be wholly alive. He, like Dede, helped me to see the beauty in the world. When he dies, I feel a piece of beauty fade along with him.

I begin developing symbols for David without realizing that is what I am doing. Soon after his death I am in a department store and stumble upon a necklace with two images on the pendant: a cross and the Virgin Mary. I buy it on instinct, and know it is for him. Christian iconography becomes an important tether to him for me, though I cannot discern why. I simply accept it, trusting that anything that makes me feel closer to him is good, is right.

I start seeing him in the flowers. I start seeing him in the meadows. I start seeing him everywhere, because I have to, in order to dry the tears.

Flowers have always been the only thing I am good at sketching.

I can doodle flowers for hours, all different kinds. I am good at drawing flowers because every flower that ever was is imperfect, and so beautiful. This is an art form I can replicate.

One day in my dorm room, I doodle a simple flower on the soft skin of my left inner wrist. It is the simplest flower I draw, a single circle in the center, with five petals radiating from it. The petals curve, and then point out. I love the look of it on my body, can feel David's energy radiating through it. I decide, let me keep this here for a while.

I do what so many college students have done before me and pull out a needle, thread, and black India ink. I get to work. I spend hours tracing my drawing with needle and ink, pressing it into my skin. I look at my wrist now, trace the outline of the petals with my finger. It is a reminder that from pain can stem beauty. It is a reminder that I can choose where I place beauty in the world. I want to place it everywhere.

One day I have a picnic with David's childhood best friend, Alexa. I have known about her since he passed, surreptitiously looked at her posts about him for comfort, for the love of it all. I knew about her since he died, but we do not meet for quite some time after that. I am nervous to spend time with her one-on-one. I am scared to be so close to someone who was so close to him. I am scared to dredge up old pain.

We go to the grocery store in Union Square and fashion a picnic feast, the way only two girls in their early twenties can. We buy a fresh loaf of bread and fancy cheese. We find freshly prepared salads and snag those too. At the bakery counter we carefully arrange an assortment of macarons for dessert. We grab some fruit and beverages for good measure, and we are on our way.

We walk down Fifth Avenue to Washington Square Park and spread our array of goodies on the ground. Alexa, a film photographer, snaps pictures of me with macarons in my mouth. We smile, we laugh, we soak up the sunshine into our skin. And then we talk about David.

I was afraid to talk about him, afraid of pain, but my fears were unwarranted. It's all love, all beauty. I am touched, immensely, by Alexa's stories of him. She knew him for so much longer and better than I did—we only met my freshman year of college. She speaks of him and brings him to life, and I see: everyone lives on in the hearts of those they love. Really, truly, lives on.

We talk about symbols. We talk about the ways we see him in the world. She tells me about an experience she had talking to a psychic medium about him. She has a recording of it on her phone and so we sit in the grass, one earbud each, and we listen. We listen to this medium talk about our friend, about how to find him in the world. Balloons, she says. You'll find him in the balloons.

We finish listening and look up. Standing next to us are two men carrying huge handfuls of balloons. They offer some to us, and we burst out laughing. We accept, and I grasp them, Alexa snapping more photographs of me. We laugh and laugh. The universe is always holding us, always moving with us.

We gather up our picnic supplies and go for a walk. Not a few blocks down the street, we see another huge plume of balloons, this time attached outside a gym for some grand opening. Without thinking, we use the knife from our picnic and slice off a couple of balloons, running down the streets, helium bandits on the go. A day I feared would be full of sadness is instead full of beauty, full of laughter and lightness. Because we made it so.

There are always balloons in the air, flowers in the ground, butterflies on petals. We can see them, appreciate them as they are. That can be enough. But we are also allowed to let these things be more. I choose to see more.

Pennies become an important symbol for David, and then again later for Dede. I know that coins are a classic way to recognize the dead, and it is because they are like butterflies: abundant.

I explain this to the man I am dating at the time, how every penny I see is a symbol for my friend. He mocks this, looks at me with pity in his eyes. Scoffs a bit. I can tell he thinks it is immature, silly. "Do you *really* think he leaves pennies for you?"

Do I *really* think he is calling out to me with coins on a sidewalk? No. Do I choose to be reminded every day on every street corner of his presence, his personhood, his impact on my life, simply because I can be? Absolutely.

I think so many of the stories we tell are ways to process the world around us. It's what I'm doing here. This whole book is an attempt to make the world more beautiful with words, with a lens. I see beauty everywhere I go, and I want to spread that, want you to see it, too. Everything is up to our interpretation, and interpretation is one of the few things in this life that we actually have a say in. Let us find abundance, beauty. Let us see a hello from a dead friend or grandmother. Let us see.

I think about astrology, tarot—tools that ground me. I turn to tarot especially in moments of uncertainty, pull a card or two and see what randomness the universe might provide. It's not that I necessarily think any one symbol, any one tarot card, any one butterfly, is absolute truth. It's more that I believe they can show us truths, can allow us to look at ourselves and the world in a different way. A practice, a story, like tarot, like butterfly searching, lets the practitioner see herself through a randomized lens. And what is that, if not holding up a kaleidoscope to nature, to ourselves?

I believe in randomness, in the power of randomness to heal. I love shuffling songs, seeing which one plays first, seeing what it has to tell me. I love flipping through random pages in a book, stopping suddenly and pointing to a sentence. Whatever I read in that bout of randomness, I let it guide me.

I think the universe is always speaking—through coincidence, through randomness, through butterflies and pennies and smiles between strangers. I think the universe is always speaking, and we can listen. We can speak back.

I used to think it was naïve to believe in more. In an afterlife, in spirituality, in anything beyond human intelligence. Now I see that to believe is not to be unintelligent or unscientific. To believe in the beauty of the world is to take the universe in our hands and decide what shades to paint it with. We can let the world be drab and sad in our eyes or we can decide that absolutely everything is full of beauty. We can seek beauty out, find it in every corner, spread it. Let it all be reminders of love.

A year or so after he dies, I have a dream about David. One that feels so real. I enter a forest, and it is dark and green. The green is almost black, and I should be afraid, but I am not. I am held. I walk deeper into the forest, and I know he is here, waiting for me. When we see each other, no words are spoken between us. No words need to be. He shows me: *I am okay here, amongst the trees.* He shows me this silently. I feel it in my bones. He is safe. He is okay.

Months ago, I am driving down a street in the next town over. I spy a massive purple buddleja. This time, I know what to look for. Sure enough, there they are: swaths of butterflies in many shades, flitting around the shrub. When I look for beauty, when I look for love, when I look for reminders that I am not alone: I can always find them.

I hate saying that everything happens for a reason, and I don't think it's true that it does. Because if it does, then what is the purpose, and whose? I do not know that there is predetermined reason for events. I do not know that there is necessity, purpose to be found in someone dying young, or dying at all. What I know is, things happen, constantly, and it is our choice how we move forward from these occurrences.

Life happens, randomly, and we assign meaning to it, and stories, and we create patterns and beauty in the randomness. That's what life is, I think, mostly. Random. So absurd, so random, and simultaneously so gorgeous and perfect and beyond reason. I am amazed every day by the random beauty, by every person, plant, animal, and sparkling piece of pavement I encounter.

I get the idea to write this book, to begin writing again at all, because I see a chipmunk at work one day. I am raking leaves by the shrubs, by the buddleja, and I see this chipmunk and I want to know: what's your story, little guy? I go home that day, and I begin to write.

I had not written in a while, had felt uninspired and devoid of anything to say. But when I see this little chipmunk, when I realize I want to know his story, tell his story, I pick up my pen.

As I begin crafting a tale of this little chipmunk and his family and his life at the garden center, I realize that this is not the story I want to tell. The story I want to tell, have told you here, is my own. I decide to write the story of this year, so that I may leave it here. So that I may move beyond it. So that perhaps one day you will be reading these words and they will inspire you to find beauty, to create beauty of your own. I am leaving this here for you, the way I dropped ink into my skin and sometimes leave pennies on the ground: so that others may see beauty of my creation. So that others may feel loved and held by the universe the way I do.

I realize now that I have hardly thanked him, that little chipmunk, for inspiring me to write again. Thank you, little guy. Thank you for existing, here, with me.

I could have seen that chipmunk scurry by, his cheeks full of food for the winter, and I could have just thought, okay, there's a chipmunk. On countless other days that's exactly what I did. But on this day, something about the way the leaves were falling and the way this particular animal looked at me, something about it all felt like the universe speaking. Something about it all felt like a butterfly in my ear, telling me to write.

Every other essay I have known how to end, have written the endings before the beginnings, except for this one. This one, I leave open, unfinished. I do not know where the future leads for me, for our planet, for all those I love. I do not know what next year brings, next week, even the next minute. All I know is I am here, now. I am surrounded by green. Butterflies live in the air. I have love in my heart. There is no end here, and no beginning, just me and you and our Mother Nature, within a story of love that we are always writing.

Reminders to myself as I complete this project, and to anyone else who may read this:

1. You deserve to share your words and ideas with the world. Your thoughts are valuable and necessary.
2. You do not have to be afraid of the judgment of others, of this work or of your personhood. Remember that you can always access your center, can always find your true self. Find her in moments when you lose sight of who you are, when you let the voices of others cloud your own.
3. If you forget where your center lives, just ask your body. Get real quiet and ask your body nicely where your true self is. She will reveal herself to you. Be patient. Vulnerability is worth waiting for. So is truth.
4. You will never be complete. I don't mean this to say you won't know peace, or won't know joy. I just mean that this journey called life is not done until it's done. You won't be complete until the process is complete, and you won't exactly be awake for that part. So just trust that it's okay to always be learning, until the very last breath. Trust that there is beauty in letting go of the need to be right, or good. Just be, and learn. Incomplete, uncertain, alive.
5. Love and give, freely and generously. It is hard to break from the notion of giving with expectation, loving with the

same. I am constantly learning to be better in this. Remember that the plants are here to teach you. They can show you how to love freer, how to give more, anytime you need a lesson.

6. Remember that your duty here, on this Earth, is to exist. To be. To soak in the beauty around you. Remember that it is okay, and right, and good, and healing (for yourself, for everyone), to pause. Stay still, get silent. Just feel, just be.

7. There is always a home for you amongst the trees. You always have a home, and you can always grow another.

8. Remember that you are a body before you are a mind. Remember that you are Nature, before you are human. There is no separating any of these parts. There is only destroying, or saving, us all. The choice is ours.

9. Remember to sow as many seeds as you can, in the Earth and in the hearts of everyone you meet. Seeds are abundant, and generative. Let them multiply.

10. Remember who you are. Remember that there is space in the soil for us all.

Acknowledgments

WRITING THIS book has been one of the most healing and moving experiences of my life. While it was written by my hand, this project would not be possible without the love and support of a multitude of people. We all wrote this.

Thank you first and foremost to my family. Thank you to my sister, Carrie Amicucci. Your presence is a gift, and has been a source of levity throughout this year. Spending time with you brought so much joy to my life amidst grief, and so much inspiration to this book as well. Thank you to my aunt, Mary Chard, for your supportive feedback on my essays. Your kind words meant so much to me. Thank you also for caring for Dede and Papa John over the years, and so selflessly; you inspired "Aloe," and you inspire me. Thank you to another aunt, Mary Amicucci, for your encouragement of this project and for your love. You have always helped me to see the beauty in my own being, and you have aided in my growth and this book more than you know. Thank you to my dad, Joseph Amicucci, for allowing me into your garden this year and for teaching me. You are such a beautiful human. Know that I try to embody your kindness and your gentle spirit every day of my life. Know that none of this would be possible without you. Thank you to my mom, Laura Amicucci, for all that you do and all that you are. Know that I think you are an incredible mother. Know that I would not change a moment of our history, because it has brought us here. I love where we are, and I love you. Thank you for nurturing my love of writing, and for nurturing me. Thank you for being Dede-like, and then some.

Thank you to my friends, all of whom I love and admire deeply. Thank you to Darcy Glastonbury, for not only encouraging this project through its duration, but also for your helpful edits on "Perennials." I love your mind, and I am so thankful that you share your brilliance with me. Being your friend reminds me every day that life is full of miracles; you are one of them. Thank you to Gabe Kawugule, for all the beauty you bring into my life, and for reminding me in the moments I need it that I can do absolutely anything. Thank you for the constant flow of art and music and fashion and gorgeousness that is your being. I am so honored by your love. Thank you to Daria Egorova, for your friendship and for your thoughts on my essays. You remind me not to take life too seriously, to find laughter everywhere, and I am so lucky to have you in my life. You are a healer, in every sense of the word, and it is inspiring to watch you find yourself in that role. Thank you to Federica Soccal. You told me while I was working on this project that you see me as *un albero saggio*—a wise tree—and hearing this filled my soul. That is what you always do: you fill my soul. You make me believe my thoughts matter; you make me feel alive and whole, seen and loved. Thank you to Nora Kyrkjebø. Being friends with you is one of the greatest joys of my life, and I am so thankful to have spent so much time with you over the last year. Thank you for reading my essays and for making me feel like my words are beautiful. Thank you for sharing your precious and splendid spirit with me. Thank you to Alexa Penn, for your reply to "Buddleja." Reading your response was the perfect circular ending to this whole project. The squirrel and the chipmunk were in on it together, laughing alongside us. Thank you for your vision of the world, and thank you for all the beauty you bring into it. Thank you to Adrian Blackman, for challenging me to think in new ways and for encouraging me to reach my fullest potential in every facet of life. Thank you for your kindness, your wisdom, your beauty, and your love. This book and I are the better for knowing you. Thank you to Anna Clare Blum. You inspire me every day to be more creative. Thank you for your endless encouragement of my writing, both inside and outside of this book. Thank you for always being there to remind me of my value, my worth, my truth. Thank you for being my friend.

Thank you to the women of Colonial Gardens, who have gifted me the knowledge that lines every page of this book. Thank you to DeeDee Faile, for the laughter, the lessons, and all you have done to help me grow. It has been a delight to get to know you this year. Thank you to Lee Proctor. Thank you for the handmade journal that inspired me to continue writing. Thank you for the late-night phone calls and text sessions on every possible topic. Thank you for reading my essays, and telling me they are meaningful and good. Thank you for your teachings and your love. Thank you to Bonnie Pfann. Thank you for taking a chance on me. Thank you for teaching me with such patience, for answering every question of mine with excitement and care. You have given me so much, and I am eternally grateful to you. All three of you have transformed my life. Thank you, thank you, thank you.

Thank you to Mikki Baloy, one of the most remarkable healers I have ever worked with. Thank you for reminding me of my own wisdom and for always guiding me in a manner that feels organic, loving, and generative. You have been a blessing in my life and have taught me so much about what it means to be human, amongst all the other people.

Thank you to my brilliant editor, Marni MacRae, for helping to make my ideas and voice shine, and for your deeply kind commentary on my essays. Your thoughts were such a validating piece of this process, and I am so thankful that you shared them with me. Thank you to my remarkable designer, Wayne Kehoe, for bringing the entirety of this book to life with kindness and care.

Thank you to you, the reader, for opening your heart to my

ideas. The impetus for this project has been to share my love of plants, and their healing capacity, with others. By reading my words, you have helped me achieve my purpose. Thank you. Have a blessed life.

About the Author

ELEANOR AMICUCCI is a Connecticut native currently residing in Rome. She has no idea what she is doing with her life (in the best way). She is probably planting seeds somewhere, and hopes you will, too. *Soon I'll Be from the Soil Someday* is her first book.